HOMEMADE

CLARKSON POTTER / PUBLISHERS

New York

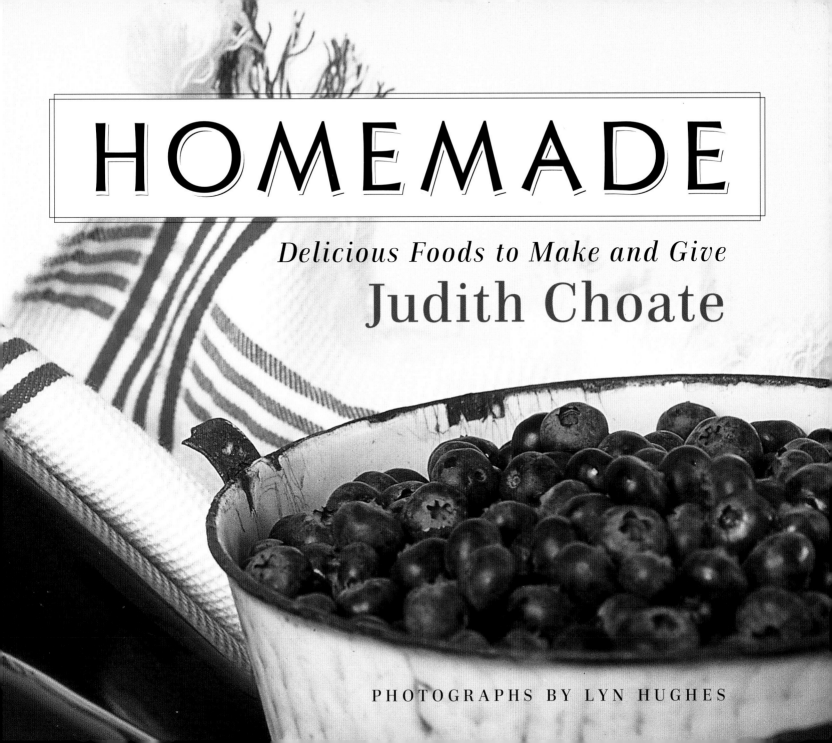

HOMEMADE

Delicious Foods to Make and Give

Judith Choate

PHOTOGRAPHS BY LYN HUGHES

Additional photography by Steve Pool
on pages 5, 10, 13, 14, 16, 25, 27 (top), 41, 55, 57,
65, 92, 93, 99, 103 (bottom), 112, 124, 134, 158, 160 (left)

Published by Clarkson Potter/Publishers, New York, New York.
Member of the Crown Publishing Group, a division of Random House, Inc.
www.crownpublishing.com

CLARKSON N. POTTER is a trademark and POTTER and colophon are
registered trademarks of Random House, Inc.

Printed in Singapore

Design by Joel Avirom and Jason Snyder
Design Assistant: Meghan Day Healey
Prop Stylist: Aris Mixon

Library of Congress Cataloging-in-Publication Data
Choate, Judith.
    Homemade : delicious foods to make and give / Judith Choate.
    1. Baking. 2. Confectionery. 3. Canning and preserving. I. Title.
    TX765.C4723 2004
    641.5—dc22   2003021574

ISBN 1-4000-5049-9

10 9 8 7 6 5 4 3 2 1

First Edition

For my homemade treasures,
Canada, Alexander, and Clara Grace Choate

Contents

ACKNOWLEDGMENTS

IT IS ONE THING TO SPEND AN AFTERNOON IN YOUR KITCHEN making a few treats to wrap and give. It is quite another to make so many of your favorite recipes at one time and then pack them beautifully to pose for the camera's eye. So I had to call on many friends, relatives, and kissin' cousins to lend a helping hand so that the book I had hoped to create could come alive on its pages. My deepest thanks go to all of the following people who helped make this book possible.

There are four firsts on my list—my husband, Stephen Pool, my sons, Michael and Christopher Choate, and my collaborator, Joel Avirom. Steve because he is always and forever my Mr. Sweetie. Mickey and Chris because they were there the first time around watching me cook with my dear friend Jane Green for *The Gift-Giver's Cookbook* and have never strayed far from the kitchen or my heart. And Joel because he never fails to be supportive and enthusiastic about all of my projects even when we have to break into our piggy banks to make them happen.

Lyn Hughes has my eternal gratitude for her fantastic eye, which fully realized the book that Joel and I had created in our mind's eye. Our thanks to Julie Kramer, also.

Aris Mixon, the dearest friend anyone could hope for and a superb stylist, lent his sense of style as well as many items from his personal collection and assisted every day in making our packages as interesting and accessible as we could have wished.

The "kids," Jason Snyder and Meghan Day Healey, perfectionists to the nth degree, seem to be able to read our minds in the design studio. You are the best!

My daughter-in-law, Laurel, who has inherited the cookie cutters that were once my mom's and then mine, keeps the spirit of giving going in the Choate house.

And my best pal, Jane Green—can it really have been so many years ago that we shared recipes and babysitting chores? You don't look a day older.

A particular thank you to Roy Finamore, whose enthusiasm for things homemade made the book a possibility.

To Adina Steiman at Clarkson Potter—I appreciate your good cheer and diligent work to realize the project as I had wished.

Cathy Green's shopping techniques translated borrowing a cup of sugar from the neighbor to borrowing pieces of equipment and treasured objects from distant companies and local retailers. Next time, you can have a credit card!

Debbie and Bruce Tarbell, the best country neighbors, picked fruit and berries with us and generously shared their garden with us.

Dr. T'nette Kuzminski led us on our first forage for wild mushrooms.

Friends, private collectors, antique dealers, and casual acquaintances lent a helping hand as well as generously allowing us into their pantries and collections. Special thanks must go to Linda and Michel Arnaud, Patty and Vinny Bocchino, Lou and Carole Carmona, Eddie Criscuolo and Richard Haney, Mary King and Tim Aberts, Lynn Marsh and Doug Delong, Mike and Margaret McMahon (with Mickey, Toots, and Beagleman), Janet and Art Dudley, Kris Kruid and Jacques Torres, Brenda and Bill Michaels of the Fly Creek Cider Mill in Fly Creek, New York, Charlie Palmer and the staff at Aureole Restaurant, Ron and Priscilla Richley, John Smith, and Betty Jo Steel of Steel's Gourmet Foods.

INTRODUCTION

WHEN MY CHILDREN WERE VERY YOUNG—and so was I—I'd spend hours in the kitchen baking, canning, creating candies and treats, and putting meal after meal, made from scratch, on the table. Even though it was the beginning of the women's liberation movement, my own strong sentiments about the equality of women could not urge me out of my beloved kitchen. I simply loved to cook. And equal to cooking, I loved to feed people and then send them home with goodie bags.

When holidays came, my kitchen was hectic with preparations for treats for the house and for gift-giving to friends, family, and business associates. One year, I, with my mom's help, made more than two thousand cookies, one hundred pounds of candy, and enough cakes and fruit breads to feed a small army. This was on top of the fifty fruitcakes that had been aging in the closet since the previous fall for the year's holiday giving and the additional fifty we had made in November to begin aging for the next year's season. All of this fevered activity took place not in a big farm kitchen but in a New York City apartment's small and very basic kitchen.

As time rolled by and my love of cooking turned into a full-time career, I found fewer opportunities to re-create the kitchen bounty of my family's early years. Besides, eating habits had changed and everyone was always on a diet or watching what they ate or forsaking meat or sugar or fat or, it sometimes seemed, even fun. I was eating in the world's finest restaurants more and more and at home less and less. I still loved to cook but found that I had very little time to spend in the kitchen except on work-related projects. I still made jams and jellies in the summer, baked bread once a week, and put sweets on the table when company came. Chutneys and condiments were jarred as the spirit moved me or when I purchased too much at the farmer's market. Nevertheless, I didn't think I would ever pack in the stores that had once filled my apartment kitchen.

However, some years ago, I too had to change the way I eat and went back into the kitchen to develop tasty recipes that would fulfill my family's needs yet still meet my medically imposed dietary requirements. At the same time, I began a new career developing chef-related food products for the commercial marketplace. Once my feet were planted back in front of the stove and over the mixer, blender, and chopping block, the creative juices begin to flow. Once again, I was making enough to feed a small army, but with my husband and me alone in the house, I had to find an outlet for my bounty.

This time I *was* in a big kitchen in the country, where friends and neighbors crowded around our large wooden dining table at least three times a week. I began buying boxes of old canning jars at auction to have useful containers on hand to fill with leftovers or something new I was developing so I could send guests on their way with take-home goodies. And what I found is that, over the years, some things had not changed very much at all. No matter how busy our lives or how steeped in technology, health concerns, or culinary trends, my friends and acquaintances still loved to be fed and nurtured with gifts from the kitchen.

Although we can now purchase almost anything premade, packaged, and delivered to the door, I believe people still know the difference between homemade and store-bought—and they welcome and truly value the real thing. So often cooks make the effort to prepare a meal from scratch and then use purchased breads, jams, condiments, vinaigrettes, or sauces. Homemade foods are often the element of surprise that greatly enhances a meal. A simple piece of grilled meat—even a basic hamburger—becomes a gourmet's treat when served with homemade Blueberry Catsup (page 133) or Asian Barbecue Sauce (page 147). Through the years, I have always found that even the simplest homemade food gift is received with pleasure.

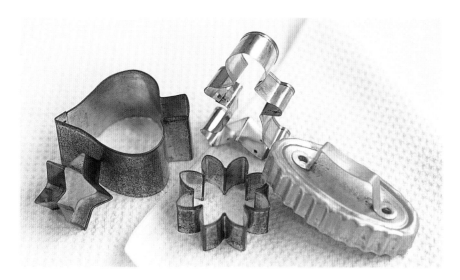

What has changed is that the home cook now has many, many more ingredients at hand from which to create interesting, personalized foods. Farmers markets abound, even in large urban areas; exotic produce is stacked high in supermarkets and specialty food stores; ethnic ingredients are available from small local markets or often on the supermarket shelf; and luxury foodstuffs are little more than an email away from any kitchen. All of this expands the larder in ways unimaginable just a few years ago.

Of course, cooking has also changed over the years. We use less animal protein, far less butter and nonvegetable oils; we serve more fresh or lightly cooked fruits and vegetables; condiments, sauces, and gravies are often fruit- or vegetable-based; fish has moved from the freezer and the can to fresh from the sea; many once-ethnic-only ingredients are now integrated into everyday dishes; and Sugar Busters is more than just a fad. These all work in combination with the cook's ingenuity to bring balance and creativity to new or refined recipes added to the homemade food gift repertoire.

Working on this book made me ever more aware that what goes around, comes around. My very first cookbook, written more than thirty years ago with my closest friend, Jane Green, was called *The Gift-Giver's Cookbook*. In it, we put together some of the recipes that had been most welcomed by friends and family. Now, here I am, all these years later, putting together recipes I have found most successful as gifts from my contemporary kitchen. Some of them have evolved from recipes used by my grandmothers, aunts, and mother or first created with Jane, others come straight from the fusion menus of today's four-star restaurants, and many were derived from the development work I have been doing in my working kitchen. However, as I read through the dog-eared pages of *Gift-Giver's,* the sentiments we expressed as young housewives resonate still: "There is almost no limit to the variety of gifts that you and your kitchen can produce. . . . Sharing the rewards of many hours in our kitchens is the nicest way of saying 'We're friends.'"

A gift of food is shown to its best advantage when it is artfully packaged. Just as you think not only about the flavors of a meal but also how it is going to look on the plate, so should you think about how to beautifully present a gift of homemade food. Of course, the canning jar holding jams, jellies, or other preserves makes an instant statement about its origins (have you noticed how many companies pack their goods in old-fashioned canning jars?), but even those jars can do with a little extra perking up. With very little effort, all the work you have done in the kitchen can be presented to great effect.

Before you begin the final wrapping, it is important that every home-made gift be labeled with its name, date of preparation, and, if necessary, a tag giving cooking or serving instructions. Although many types of decorative labels can be purchased, you can also make your own personalized labels on a computer. I find that stick-on labels are the most reliable and prefer them to those that have to be tied or glued on.

There is no end to decorative labels, papers, fabrics, boxes, ribbons, and containers that can help turn your homemade wares into extra-special gifts. Use your imagination along with felt-tip pens, crayons, or colored pencils, computer graphics, rubber stamps, and decorative papers to create distinctive designs and wraps. If you have children, let them participate in preparing the final package—very often their simple approach is just what the package needs to make its point.

I save decorative bottles and jars all year long. Many imported vinegars, oils, and condiments come packed in beautiful and unusual containers that are easily reused. It is fun to buy old containers at auctions, flea markets, and thrift shops. Whenever an unusual tin, container, crock, or box catches my eye, I purchase it to have on hand for the perfect gift package.

Plastic film, aluminum foil, disposable foil or paper baking pans, and paper goods make packaging and transporting cakes and breads quite simple. Most baked goods stay fresher if they are first tightly wrapped in plastic film or cellophane and sealed closed. Some cakes and breads look perfectly fine wrapped in aluminum foil, sealed with stick-on seals, and tied with a pretty cloth ribbon. Others require a little imagination to make an appealing gift package.

Clear plastic containers often make an attractive and useful gift in addition to the brightly wrapped cake or bread loaves you can put in them. Cardboard cake plates (see Resources, page 170) make a great base for round cakes or breads. You can also use an antique or thrift shop plate as a base so the recipient gets two gifts in one. For important gifts, you might want to place the cake on a beautiful cake plate or the bread in an attractive new or antique breadbox or basket.

Cookies are easily given in almost any covered container, ranging from a shoe box covered with decorative paper to reusable new or antique tins or cookie jars. With a little imagination, restaurant-sized mayonnaise or pickle jars can be painted or trimmed and used as cookie jars. Always pack cookies carefully, in layers, separated by colorful tissue, cellophane, foil, or waxed paper.

Cookies also lend themselves to being packed with baking utensils as a wedding or shower gift or as a housewarming gift for newlyweds or for someone setting up a first apartment. A flour sifter, measuring cups and spoons, cookie sheets, mixing bowls and spoons—any or all of these holding a pound or two of cookies shows you have taken the time to create a special gift.

Children, of course, find homemade cookies a real treat, but they love them even more when they arrive in a special container—inexpensive sandbox toys, plastic trucks, and carrying cases all work well.

Gift containers for candy and nuts can be almost any size or shape. I often reuse cans that have plastic snap-on lids such as those in which you purchase nuts, ground coffee, and snacks. These can be spray-painted or covered with decorative self-stick papers or kraft paper on which stickers or free-form designs have been placed. Oatmeal and cornmeal containers and shallow plastic pans are also terrific for this purpose. Another charming container is easily made by covering a paper-towel tube with colorful decorative paper, sealing one end, filling it with candy or nuts, and then sealing the second end closed by cutting a circle about 1 inch larger than the opening and tying it over the opening with a cloth ribbon. Again, antique or junk-store finds often make handy containers for sweets.

Canning jars can simply be labeled and given as is, but I often jazz them up by cutting circles (with pinking shears) of colorful fabric somewhat larger than the lids and screwing the fabric circle under the outer ring to make a fancy hat or by trimming the lids with raffia or yarn. A more elaborate garnish is to glue beans, seeds, or spices to the lid; this works only when the trim reflects the contents of the jar. The jars themselves can also be decorated with colored plastic tape or paint, but unless you have nothing else to do, this is really gilding the lily.

When packaging sauces, vinaigrettes and dressings, snacks, and other foods in canning jars or resealable plastic bags, try to use containers appropriate to the item or have some use on the table. For dry mixes, colorful drawstring bags can also be used. When giving something that is a bit exotic or has a particular ethnic spin, make sure your label gives serving or cooking instructions just in case the recipient is unfamiliar with the food.

Using a mixture of homemade gifts from your kitchen, you can put together marvelous baskets for housewarmings, cocktail parties, showers—in fact, for almost any occasion. Begin with a beautiful basket, gather homemade gifts that go together—jams, jellies, breads, and butters; relishes, pickles, chutneys, and seasonings; savory sauces and appetizers—add a couple of household items—kitchen utensils, cocktail napkins and picks, unusual serving utensils, and so forth—and pack the container chock-a-block with bright tissue and trimmings. Pull cellophane—clear or colored—up and around the basket and tie a big, fat bow on the handle. What better present could you buy? You don't have to shout "I made it myself!" if you take care to present your homemade wares with the same attention you gave to making them.

■   ■   ■

No matter how tasty your homemade gift, if it is poorly packed and reaches its destination broken, crumbled, or spilled, it won't have a chance to shine.

Cakes, breads, and tea breads should be wrapped in foil or plastic film, labeled, and then gift-wrapped. With the exception of long-lasting fruitcakes, most cakes should not be shipped unless they are sent for overnight delivery on the day they were baked or shipped frozen for express delivery. It does help to wrap the gift-wrapped item or box in a triple layer of newspaper with at least an inch of shredded paper, styrofoam peanuts, or other packing material in the bottom of the shipping box and around the sides and top of the gift. Mark the shipping box PERISHABLE and HANDLE WITH CARE.

Bar and drop cookies are the best long-haul shippers. Almost all other cookies are fine for local giving. Either way, it is best to either wrap each cookie individually in plastic film or carefully pack the cookies in a sturdy container (such as a tin) in layers, separated by colorful tissue paper, rice paper, baking sheets, or waxed paper. If shipping over a long distance, pack as for cakes and breads, allowing at least 3 inches between the tin and the shipping container.

Candies and sugar-coated nuts should be shipped long distances only when the weather is cool and dry; otherwise, even with great packing, they often change texture due to temperature fluctuations. Other nuts are generally good shippers if they are packed in a tin or other solid container and placed in a shipping box allowing at least 1 inch of space all around, with the space packed with crumpled newspaper or other packing material to keep the container stationary. All candies and nuts are terrific for local giving as long as they are packed appropriately. Candies, particularly, should be individually wrapped in plastic film to keep them from sticking together.

All foods that are preserved or packed in glass, ceramic, or other breakable containers must be packed carefully for giving. When shipping, each container should be individually wrapped in bubble wrap and surrounded by at least 1 inch of bubble wrap or foam packing materials. There should also be at least 2 inches of insulation all around the interior of the shipping box, which itself should be well wrapped and labeled FRAGILE. For local gift-giving or when hand-delivered as a hostess gift, foods in breakable containers should always be wrapped in bubble wrap, even if they are going to be given informally in a colorful shopping bag with bright tissue sticking out of the top. This will ensure that they arrive intact even if you trip going up the steps!

When packing many types of homemade goodies in one large container or box, make sure that each has ample room and is protected from all the others. Even if you are packing a gift basket, use an abundance of tissue paper, cellophane, or other decorative wrap to protect your wares. This way, if something breaks, spills, or crumbles, the entire package will not be ruined.

If you take time in packing, almost anything can be shipped, long distance or locally, or hand-carried to its destination. Go overboard with packing materials, using pedestrian ones for long-haul shipping and decorative ones for local delivery. This little extra effort will help your gift arrive intact.

HELPFUL HINTS

Here are just a few hints that will make the preparation of homemade gifts from your kitchen a bit easier. These simple tasks, when properly done, make the cook's job a breeze and ensure that the final taste of the gift will be absolutely wonderful.

- Before beginning any recipe, make sure you have all of the ingredients and utensils required, measure out the appropriate amounts, and prepare all equipment. Once this is done, the preparation will move quickly ahead.

- Nuts, which are quite oily, need a bit of care when toasting to keep them from burning and turning bitter. They may be toasted in a skillet over medium-low heat or in a preheated 300°F oven. If toasting in the oven, place the nuts in a single layer on a parchment paper-lined baking pan. On the stovetop, stir the nuts frequently and in the oven, toss after baking for 5 minutes; then check often to prevent scorching. Nicely toasted nuts are lightly colored and very aromatic. Fresh coconut and other spices may be toasted using either of these methods. However, coconut will toast more evenly in the oven, while spices do best when toasted on top of the stove.

- Raw or toasted nuts can often be purchased ground. However, to ensure freshness, I always grind nuts in my own kitchen in the small bowl of a food processor fitted with a metal blade. This can also be done in an old-fashioned manual nut grinder or by chopping with a very sharp chef's knife. Whatever method you use, take care that the nuts are not pulverized and mushy.

- Ginger juice is now available at specialty food stores and some Asian markets. If you cannot find it, you can make it by puréeing fresh, peeled ginger root in a food processor fitted with a metal blade or grating it on a box or Asian ginger grater and then pressing the puréed or grated ginger through cheesecloth or a fine-mesh sieve to squeeze out the juice.

- Solid chocolate can be melted in a microwave oven or in the top half of a double boiler over simmering water. Melt slowly and carefully because chocolate scorches easily.

- Roasted garlic purée as well as whole roasted cloves can now be purchased in most supermarkets and specialty food stores. However, homemade is much better. Lightly coat either unpeeled whole garlic heads or peeled individual cloves with olive oil, wrap them in aluminum foil, and place them on a baking pan in a preheated 350°F oven. Whole heads will take about 25 minutes and individual cloves about 12 minutes to become soft and aromatic. To make garlic purée, roast whole heads and, when they are done, unwrap them, cut off the tops, and squeeze out the soft flesh. One large head usually yields about 2 tablespoons garlic purée.

- Bell peppers may be roasted over an open flame on top of the stove or under the broiler. Turn the peppers frequently until all of the skin is blackened. Place the peppers in an airtight plastic bag and allow to steam for about 15 minutes, then remove the peppers from the bag and push off the charred skin.

- Roast dried chile peppers in a heavy-duty frying pan over medium heat. Using tongs, turn the chiles often until all sides are browned slightly and the flesh is somewhat softened. Most roasted dried chiles are not peeled, but their stems and seeds are usually removed.

■   ■   ■

HOMEMADE

1

ALL KINDS OF CAKES

Almost all cake directions begin with the words "Cream butter and sugar until light and fluffy." This is one of the most important steps for successful cake making. If you begin with butter that is at room temperature, it will be properly creamed into the sugar when the sugar has lost its graininess, the color is quite pale, and the mixture fluffs when lifted with a spoon. If these two basic ingredients are improperly creamed, the result will be a tough cake.

All of the cakes I have chosen may be prepared in advance and frozen. To prepare cakes for freezing, wrap them in plastic film and then wrap them carefully in freezer paper, seal with freezer tape, label, and mark with the date of baking. It is best not to freeze cakes for longer than three months, as they will begin to lose flavor. You can frost or glaze the cake before or after freezing. I prefer to frost after a frozen cake has thawed (unwrapped, for about an hour), as the frosting or glaze will often sweat as it thaws. The taste will be fine, but the cake won't look quite as nice. Most of the cakes featured in this section can be served either as is or with a glaze or frosting, if desired.

Be sure to choose the finest-quality ingredients available to you. Freshly ground spices, pure extracts, organic fruits and nuts, premium butter and chocolate, and unbleached flours are but a few of the ingredients that will ensure the best-tasting cake. All of these top-notch ingredients are readily available at specialty food stores, some supermarkets, by mail order, and on the Internet.

The recipes list the necessary equipment as well as any special requirements. It is important to use the same measuring utensils for each ingredient, as there is often a difference between sets of measuring cups and spoons. For dry ingredients, you will want to use measuring cups and spoons that correspond to the exact amount called for in the recipe. For liquids, well-marked glass measuring cups with spouts are best. Rubber spatulas, wire racks, and nonstick pans make cake baking easier. Even when using nonstick pans, I use Baker's Joy, a nonstick spray with flour, to facilitate removing the cake from the pan. I have found that other nonstick vegetable sprays do not work as well and, in fact, tend to leave a residue in the pan that, over time, causes buildup and reduces the nonstick properties of the pan. Plastic film, aluminum foil, and disposable pans and paper goods as well as disposable cake rounds make packaging and transporting gift cakes relatively simple. If you follow the instructions carefully, you should have no trouble creating perfect cakes that move from your kitchen to the gift box with ease.

Gift cakes can be simply placed on a cardboard cake circle and covered in plastic film or cellophane and tied with a pretty ribbon. For a longer-lasting gift, present the cake on a new or antique cake stand or in a round basket with a pretty cake knife or with some inexpensive dessert plates to receive the cut slices. No matter the style, a homemade cake is always a welcome gift.

Chocolate Malt Cake

PREHEAT OVEN TO: 350°F

UTENSILS NEEDED: Heavy-bottomed saucepan; sifter; electric mixer; one 9-inch springform tube pan, lightly buttered and floured; wire rack

BAKING TIME: Approximately 45 minutes

STORAGE: Refrigerate, wrapped in plastic film, for up to 3 days. Alternatively, freeze.

SERVING SUGGESTION: At room temperature with a dollop of whipped cream or a scoop of malted milk ice cream

---

INGREDIENTS

1 cup sweetened condensed milk

2 ounces unsweetened chocolate, chopped

2 cups sifted all-purpose flour

½ cup Dutch-process cocoa powder, sifted

2 tablespoons malted milk powder

½ cup (1 stick) unsalted butter, at room temperature

1 cup sugar

2 large eggs

1 teaspoon baking soda

1 cup milk

1 teaspoon pure vanilla extract

2 cups mini malted milk balls or 1½ cups semisweet chocolate chunks

Combine the condensed milk and unsweetened chocolate in a heavy-bottomed saucepan over medium-high heat. Stirring constantly, bring to a boil. Lower the heat and simmer, stirring constantly, for about 5 minutes or until the mixture is puddinglike. Remove from the heat and allow to cool.

Sift together the flour, cocoa, and malted milk powder. Set aside.

Place the butter in the bowl of an electric mixer and beat until slightly creamy. With the motor running, add the sugar and continue beating until the mixture is light and fluffy. Beat in the eggs, one at a time, until well blended. Beat in the cooled chocolate mixture.

Stir the baking soda into the milk and immediately add it to the batter. Then add the flour mixture, a bit at a time, beating constantly. When all of the dry ingredients have been added, fold in the vanilla and the malted milk balls, making sure the candy is well distributed throughout the batter.

Pour the batter into the prepared pan. Bake for about 45 minutes, or until the edges pull away from the sides of the pan. Remove from the oven and place on a wire rack to cool for 15 minutes. Pop the cake from the pan and continue cooling the cake on the wire rack. Serve at room temperature.

Nonfat Chocolate Cake

INGREDIENTS

2 cups nonfat plain yogurt

¼ cup Fat Replacement
  Fruit Purée (see
  opposite) or
  commercially prepared
  fat replacement such
  as Lighter Bake

1½ cups sugar

1½ cups all-purpose flour

1 cup Dutch-process cocoa
  powder

1 teaspoon baking soda

½ teaspoon baking
  powder

2 teaspoons pure vanilla
  extract

4 large egg whites, stiffly
  beaten

CHOCOLATE GLAZE
  (optional)

1 cup confectioners' sugar

3 tablespoons Dutch-
  process cocoa powder

1 teaspoon instant
  espresso powder

1½ tablespoons hot water

1 teaspoon pure vanilla
  extract

PREHEAT OVEN TO: 350°F

UTENSILS NEEDED: Electric mixer; fine-mesh sieve; one 9-inch springform cake pan, lightly sprayed with nonstick cooking spray (preferably Baker's Joy) and dusted with unsweetened cocoa powder; wire rack

BAKING TIME: Approximately 40 minutes

STORAGE: If glazed, refrigerate, wrapped in plastic film, for up to 5 days; if unglazed, refrigerate or freeze.

SERVING SUGGESTION: Unglazed, at room temperature, with a drizzle of nonfat vanilla or coffee yogurt

---

Put the yogurt and fat replacement purée in the large bowl of an electric mixer and beat to just combine. Add the sugar and beat for about 2 minutes, or until the sugar begins to dissolve.

Mix the flour, cocoa powder, baking soda, and baking powder together. Add the dry mixture to the yogurt mixture and beat until blended. Stir in the vanilla.

Gently fold the beaten egg whites into the batter to just incorporate. Scrape into the prepared pan and bake for about 40 minutes, or until a cake tester inserted into the center comes out clean.

Remove from the oven and place on a wire rack to cool.

When cool, pop the cake from the pan and transfer it to a cake plate. If using, lightly coat the top of the cake with the chocolate glaze, allowing it to drip down the sides. Serve, in small slices, at room temperature.

FOR CHOCOLATE GLAZE: Combine the sugar, cocoa powder, and espresso powder in a small bowl. Stirring constantly, drizzle in the water and vanilla and continue mixing until well blended.

If not using immediately, cover with plastic film and set aside at room temperature for no more than 1 hour.

Fat Replacement Fruit Purée

2 ripe, firm pears, well washed
2 medium apples, well washed
6 pitted dried plums
1 tablespoon lecithin granules (available at health food stores)
¾ cup water
1 tablespoon fresh lemon juice

Cut the unpeeled pears and apples into pieces. Do not core. Place in a medium saucepan along with the dried plums and lecithin. Add the water and lemon juice and stir to combine. Place over medium heat and bring to a simmer. Cook, stirring occasionally, for about 30 minutes, or until the fruit is very soft.

Remove from the heat and allow to cool for 30 minutes.

Place the mixture in a fine-mesh sieve set over a mixing bowl. Using a spatula, press against the solids to make a saucelike purée. Place in a nonreactive container, cover, and refrigerate for up to 5 days or freeze for up to 6 months. Since this recipe makes about 2 cups, divide the purée into ¼-cup servings when freezing so it can be defrosted in small amounts as needed.

Mexican Chocolate Cake

PREHEAT OVEN TO: 350°F

UTENSILS NEEDED: Double boiler; whisk; electric mixer; one 9-inch springform pan, generously buttered and dusted with cocoa powder; wire rack; fine-mesh sieve

BAKING TIME: Approximately 30 minutes

STORAGE: Refrigerate, wrapped in plastic film, for up to 3 days. Alternatively, freeze, thaw, and then dust with Dutch-process cocoa powder.

SERVING SUGGESTION: Chilled, with a dollop of cinnamon-scented whipped cream or a scoop of coffee, cinnamon, or vanilla ice cream

INGREDIENTS

- ¾ pound (12 ounces) unsweetened chocolate, broken into pieces
- 1½ cups (3 sticks) unsalted butter
- 1 tablespoon finely ground (as for Turkish coffee) espresso coffee beans
- 1 teaspoon freshly ground cinnamon
- ½ teaspoon finely ground Arbol chile powder
- 8 large eggs, separated
- 1¾ cups superfine sugar
- 2 tablespoons Kahlùa liqueur
- Approximately 2 tablespoons Dutch-process cocoa powder for dusting

Combine the chocolate and butter in the top half of a double boiler over very hot water. Heat, stirring constantly, for about 5 minutes or until the chocolate and butter melt and are well incorporated. Whisk in the ground coffee, cinnamon, and chile powder. Remove from the heat and keep warm.

Place the egg yolks in the bowl of an electric mixer and beat, on high, for about 4 minutes or until the egg yolks are very light. Beating constantly, gradually add the sugar and continue beating until the mixture falls in ribbons off the beaters. Stir in the Kahlùa. Slowly whisk the chocolate mixture into the egg yolk mixture, mixing just until blended. Set aside.

In a clean mixing bowl, beat the egg whites until stiff but not dry. Softly but thoroughly fold the egg whites into the chocolate mixture. Reserve 1 cup of the batter and pour the remaining batter into the prepared pan. Place the pan in the preheated oven and bake for about 30 minutes, or until the center is just set (the top might crack). Remove from the oven and place on a wire rack to cool.

When cool, remove the cake from the pan and turn it onto a cake plate or disposable cake round. Spread reserved chocolate batter on top of the cake as an icing, using a spatula to even the edges.

Place the cocoa powder in a fine sieve. Place the sieve above the top of the cake and, moving it over the top of the cake, gently tap the side of the sieve to dust the cake with cocoa. Transfer to the refrigerator to chill. After about 1 hour, lightly cover the cake with plastic film and chill for an additional 5 hours before serving.

Hazelnut Pound Cake

PREHEAT OVEN TO: 350°F

UTENSILS NEEDED: Electric mixer; one 10-inch tube or bundt pan, preferably nonstick, lightly buttered and dusted with Wondra flour or sprayed with nonstick cooking spray (preferably Baker's Joy), or three 9-inch loaf pans, lined with parchment paper lightly buttered and dusted with Wondra flour; wire rack

BAKING TIME: Approximately 1 hour

STORAGE: Refrigerate, wrapped in plastic film, up to 5 days. Alternatively, freeze.

SERVING SUGGESTION: At room temperature with a drizzle of hot fudge sauce and a dollop of whipped cream

---

INGREDIENTS

2 cups (4 sticks) unsalted butter, at room temperature

2 cups sugar

10 large eggs, at room temperature

4 cups sifted cake flour

2 cups chopped toasted hazelnuts (filberts)

1 tablespoon pure vanilla extract

2 teaspoons freshly grated orange zest

Place the butter in the bowl of an electric mixer and beat until very creamy. Gradually add the sugar and beat until the mixture is light and fluffy. With the motor running, add the eggs one at a time, beating well after each addition.

When the mixture is very well blended, gradually add the flour, beating to a smooth batter. Add the nuts, vanilla, and orange zest and beat to just combine. Scrape the batter into the prepared pan(s). Bake for about 45 minutes to 1 hour, or until a cake tester inserted into the center comes out clean.

Remove from the oven and invert onto a wire rack. Allow to come to room temperature before serving or storing.

Lemon-Poppy Seed Pound Cake

PREHEAT OVEN TO: 350°F

UTENSILS NEEDED: Electric mixer; one 10-inch tube or bundt pan, preferably nonstick, lightly buttered and dusted with Wondra flour or sprayed with nonstick cooking spray (preferably Baker's Joy), or three 9-inch loaf pans, lined with parchment paper lightly buttered and dusted with Wondra flour; wire rack; small nonreactive saucepan

BAKING TIME: Approximately 50 minutes

STORAGE: Refrigerate, wrapped in plastic film, up to 5 days. Alternatively, freeze.

SERVING SUGGESTION: At room temperature with a dollop of whipped cream or crème fraîche, a drizzle of lemon yogurt, or a scoop of vanilla ice cream or citrus sorbet

---

INGREDIENTS

¾ cup (1½ sticks) unsalted butter, at room temperature

1¼ cups sugar

3 large eggs

1 tablespoon freshly squeezed lemon juice

2 cups all-purpose flour, sifted

1 teaspoon baking soda

1 cup sour cream

1½ tablespoons poppy seeds

2 teaspoons freshly grated lemon zest

LEMON TOPPING

½ cup sugar

6 tablespoons freshly squeezed lemon juice

2 tablespoons orange liqueur

Place the butter in the bowl of an electric mixer and beat until just softened. Add the sugar and beat on medium speed until light and fluffy. Add the eggs, one at a time, beating well after each addition. Beat in the lemon juice.

Sift the flour and baking soda together. Gradually add the dry ingredients to the butter mixture alternately with the sour cream. When well combined, add the poppy seeds and lemon zest and stir to incorporate.

Scrape the mixture into the prepared pan(s). Bake for approximately 50 minutes for the 10-inch pan or 35 minutes for the loaf pans, or until the edges pull away from the pan and a cake tester inserted into the center comes out clean. Remove from the oven and place on a wire rack.

Prepare the Lemon Topping and, while it's still hot, pour over the cake and allow to cool. When cool, remove the cake from the pan and place on a cake plate or stand. Serve at room temperature.

FOR LEMON TOPPING: Combine the sugar and lemon juice in a small nonreactive saucepan over medium heat and bring to a simmer. Simmer, stirring constantly, for about 4 minutes or until the sugar is dissolved. Add the liqueur and cook for 1 additional minute. Remove from the heat and immediately pour over the hot cake.

Slim-Jim Carrot Cake

CHILLING TIME: 12 hours

PREHEAT OVEN TO: 350°F

UTENSILS NEEDED: Nonreactive continer with lid; large mixing bowl; electric mixer; one 10-inch tube or bundt pan, preferably nonstick, lightly buttered and dusted with Wondra flour or sprayed with nonstick cooking spray (preferably Baker's Joy); wire rack

BAKING TIME: Approximately 1 hour

STORAGE: Refrigerate, wrapped in plastic film, up to 5 days. Alternatively, freeze.

SERVING SUGGESTION: Drizzled with nonfat vanilla yogurt

INGREDIENTS

- 2 cups finely chopped carrots
- 1 cup peeled, finely chopped apples
- ½ cup finely chopped fresh pineapple
- 1 cup golden seedless raisins
- ½ cup chopped candied ginger
- 1 cup frozen apple juice concentrate
- 1 tablespoon pure vanilla extract
- 1 tablespoon freshly grated orange zest
- 2½ cups pastry flour
- 2 cups whole wheat pastry flour
- 1½ tablespoons ground cinnamon
- 1 tablespoon baking powder
- 1 teaspoon baking soda
- 1 teaspoon pumpkin pie spice
- ½ cup low-fat buttermilk
- ½ cup plain nonfat yogurt
- 3 large egg whites, stiffly beaten
- 1 cup chopped toasted walnuts or pecans, optional

Combine the carrots, apples, pineapple, raisins, and ginger in a nonreactive container with a lid. Stir in the apple juice concentrate, vanilla, and orange zest. Cover and refrigerate for 12 hours.

When the fruit has finished marinating, blend the pastry flours with the cinnamon, baking powder, baking soda, and pumpkin pie spice in a large mixing bowl. Make a well in the center and pour in the marinated fruit mixture. Stir to combine, then stir in the buttermilk and then the yogurt.

When well blended, fold in the beaten egg whites and, if using, the nuts.

Pour the batter into the prepared pan. Bake for 1 hour, or until the edges begin to pull away from the pan and a cake tester inserted into the center comes out with just a few crumbs clinging to it. Invert onto a wire rack and allow to cool before serving or storing.

Aris's Apple and Toasted Pecan Cake

PREHEAT OVEN TO: 350°F

UTENSILS NEEDED: Electric mixer; sifter; one 10-inch tube or bundt pan, preferably nonstick, lightly buttered and dusted with Wondra flour; wire rack

BAKING TIME: Approximately 1 hour

STORAGE: Refrigerate, wrapped in plastic film, up to 1 week. Alternatively, freeze.

SERVING SUGGESTIONS: At room temperature with a dollop of whipped cream, crème fraîche, or vanilla ice cream, or a drizzle of apple syrup

---

Combine the eggs with the white and brown sugars and beat until well blended. Stir in the oil, Cointreau, and vanilla and continue beating until creamy.

Sift together the flour, baking soda, cinnamon, nutmeg, and salt in a separate bowl and then blend them into the creamed mixture. Fold in the apples, pecans, and raisins. When well combined, scrape the batter into the prepared pan. Bake for approximately 1 hour, or until the edges pull away from the pan and a cake tester inserted into the center comes out with a few crumbs clinging to it.

Remove from the oven and place on a wire rack to cool for 10 minutes. Then, invert onto the wire rack and allow to cool to room temperature before serving or storing.

INGREDIENTS

3 large eggs, at room temperature

1¼ cups sugar

½ cup tightly packed light brown sugar

1½ cups canola oil

1 tablespoon Cointreau liqueur

1 teaspoon pure vanilla extract

3 cups all-purpose flour

1 teaspoon baking soda

1 tablespoon ground cinnamon

½ teaspoon freshly grated nutmeg

½ teaspoon salt

1 Gala apple, peeled, cored, and chopped

1 Fuji apple, peeled, cored, and chopped

1 Granny Smith apple, peeled, cored, and chopped

1 cup chopped toasted pecans

½ cup seedless dark raisins

Kugelhopf

¾ cup golden seedless
    raisins

3 tablespoons
    kirschwasser (cherry
    brandy), orange
    liqueur, or orange juice

1 cup lukewarm
    (115°–120°F) milk

1 package active dry yeast

¾ cup sugar

2 teaspoons pure vanilla
    extract

4 large eggs, at room
    temperature

1 teaspoon salt

Approximately 4 cups
    all-purpose flour

¾ cup (1½ sticks)
    unsalted butter, at
    room temperature,
    cut into pieces

¾ cup slivered blanched
    almonds

½ cup diced mixed
    candied fruit

15–20 blanched whole
    almonds

Confectioners' sugar,
    optional

PREHEAT OVEN TO: 350°F (Note that much preparation must take place before preheating.)

UTENSILS NEEDED: Small bowl; heavy-duty electric mixer with a dough hook; kugelhopf pan or 9-inch bundt pan, lightly buttered; wire rack

RISING TIME: Approximately 4 hours

BAKING TIME: Approximately 1 hour

STORAGE: Keep at room temperature, wrapped in plastic film, 1 day. Alternatively, refrigerate up to 3 days, or freeze.

SERVING SUGGESTION: Serve slightly warm or at room temperature

———————————

Place the raisins in a small bowl. Add the kirschwasser and set aside for 1 hour.

Place the lukewarm milk and yeast in the bowl of a heavy-duty mixer fitted with the dough hook. Stir on low until the yeast is dissolved. Add the sugar and vanilla and beat to just blend. Stop the mixer and let the mixture stand for about 5 minutes, or until foamy. When foamy, add the eggs, one at a time, and beat well after each addition.

Stir the salt into the flour and gradually add the flour until almost all of it is incorporated into the yeast mixture. The dough will be sticky and elastic.

With the motor running, add the butter, 1 piece at a time, kneading each piece into the dough. After all of the butter is incorporated, continue kneading for another 10 minutes, adding flour as needed until the dough does not stick to the dough hook. Beat in the reserved raisins, their soaking liquid, the slivered almonds, and the candied fruit.

Remove the bowl from the mixer stand. Cover and place in a warm spot for about 2 hours, or until doubled in size.

When the dough has doubled in size, turn it out onto a lightly floured surface (Wondra flour works well). Punch down the dough and knead by hand for about 3 minutes, or until all the air pockets have burst. Return the dough to the bowl, cover, and let rest in a warm spot for about 1 hour or until again doubled in size. (Alternatively, this rise can take place overnight in the refrigerator.)

Place a whole almond in each indentation of a buttered kugelhopf mold or in a decorative pattern in the bottom of a buttered bundt pan.

Turn out the dough onto a lightly floured surface and knead by hand for 3 minutes. Shape the dough into an even cylinder that will fit nicely into the prepared pan. Place the dough in the pan, cover, and set aside in a warm spot for about 1 hour or until the dough rises almost to the top of the pan.

Uncover. Bake in the preheated oven for approximately 1 hour, or until golden brown and the edges begin to pull away from the pan.

Remove from the oven and place on a wire rack to cool for 10 minutes. Invert onto the wire rack and let cool to room temperature. If desired, dust with confectioners' sugar when cool. It's best served at room temperature after resting for 24 hours.

2

COOKIES

FOR MANY COOKS, COOKIES ARE THE EASIEST DESSERT to make. And I can't think of anything more appreciated than a box or bag of fresh-from-the-oven cookies. There are so many methods for making cookies that I have found it simplest to divide the cookies by type. Some take almost no skill to make, while a few might require a little practice to make perfect.

Good cookie-making equipment will greatly enhance your ability to easily create these little gems. Beyond the usual basic kitchen appliances, spoons and spatulas, heavy-duty nonstick cookie sheets, and wire cooling racks are essential. Even regular cookie sheets sprayed with nonstick baking spray cannot compete with fine-quality nonstick pans. If you see days of cookie making in your future, these pans are a solid investment.

A cookie press and an assortment of cookie cutters will broaden your cookie-making horizon. The latter are available in a terrific assortment of holiday, animal, and cartoon character varieties—in fact, almost any shape—from most specialty food stores, gourmet kitchenware shops and catalogs, and online. Cookie presses are available in both manual and electric models; I find the electric presses to be the most efficient and easy to use.

It is also important to have the appropriate spatula for lifting hot cookies from the nonstick baking sheet. A coated spatula made specifically for use with nonstick bakeware will keep the pans from being scratched and marred, which would reduce their nonstick quality.

When making cookies, it is important to use the exact ingredients called for in the recipe (except for chopped nuts, which can be used interchangeably, though there will be flavor differences). This is particularly important with butter; you will want to use fine-quality unsalted butter in all cases, since margarine or other fats will alter the flavor and texture of the finished cookie. However, using margarine or vegetable shortening will prolong the shelf life of any cookie.

Unless specified otherwise in a recipe, cookies can be frozen either as dough or baked. Pressed or cutout cookies may be formed into the desired shape, frozen on a cookie sheet, then removed and layered, separated by plastic film or waxed paper, and wrapped in plastic film or freezer wrap or placed in airtight plastic bags for longer freezer storage. Just be sure to label and date the package. Thaw unbaked cookies on a double layer of paper towel to absorb excess moisture before baking as directed in the specific recipe.

I have made some cookies so many times that I no longer have a recipe; I simply make them from memory. They are, of course, the most familiar cookies—chocolate chip and oatmeal raisin—that seemed to please everyone on every occasion. The cookies I have chosen here are delightfully less run-of-the-mill, yet I think they will easily find a favorite place in your repertoire.

I often pack cookies for giving in a simple brown paper bag—easy to open and easy to dispose of when the cookies quickly disappear. However, how you pack cookies for giving very much depends on the recipient. Cookies for children should be packed either simply or with whimsy. An age-appropriate toy, a reusable art bag, a backpack, or some cookie cutters accompanied with simple sugar cookies all make wonderful containers or gift additions. I've even given a simple bag of cookies with a promise of an afternoon of cookie making or gingerbread house making in my kitchen.

Dried Cherry-Almond Biscotti

PREHEAT OVEN TO: 300°F

UTENSILS NEEDED: Electric mixer; 2 nonstick baking sheets or 2 baking sheets lined
with parchment paper lightly sprayed with nonstick baking spray; wire racks

BAKING TIME: Approximately 1 hour

QUANTITY: About 3 dozen

STORAGE: Keep airtight up to 1 week. Alternatively, wrap tightly and freeze up to 3 months.

INGREDIENTS

4 ounces dried cherries

2½ cups all-purpose flour

1 cup sugar

*½ teaspoon baking
powder*

½ teaspoon baking soda

4 large eggs

*1 teaspoon almond
extract*

*1 cup whole almonds
(with skins)*

*Approximately ½ cup
Wondra flour*

Place the cherries in a small heatproof bowl. Cover with boiling water and set aside to soak for 5 minutes. When plumped, drain well and pat dry. Set aside.

Combine the flour, sugar, baking powder, and baking soda in the bowl of an electric mixer. Add 3 of the eggs along with the almond extract and slowly beat until a firm dough forms. Add the almonds with the reserved cherries and, using a wooden spoon, mix them into the dough.

Lightly coat a clean, flat surface with Wondra flour.

Place the remaining egg in a small shallow bowl. Add about 1 teaspoon cold water and whisk together to make an egg wash. Set aside.

Using your hands, scoop up the dough and place it on the lightly floured surface. Knead by hand for about 3 minutes or until the dough is somewhat pliable. Break the dough into two pieces of equal size. Form each piece into a log about 13 inches long by 2 inches wide, slightly tapering each side of the top to form the classic biscotti shape. Place the logs about 3 inches apart on a nonstick cookie sheet and, using a pastry brush, lightly coat each log with egg wash. Bake for 30 minutes. Remove the cookie sheet from the oven and place it on a wire rack for 10 minutes. Do not turn off the oven. After 10 minutes, using a spatula, transfer the logs from the cookie sheet to a clean, flat surface. Using a sharp serrated knife, cut the logs crosswise, into ¾-inch-thick slices.

Place the cookie slices, cut side down, about ½ inch apart on a nonstick cookie sheet. Return the biscotti to the oven and bake for about 20 more minutes, turning once midway so that each side is pale golden brown and the cookies are baked through. Remove from the oven and place on wire racks to cool. Serve at room temperature.

Toffee Bars

INGREDIENTS

1½ cups sifted all-purpose flour

½ cup confectioners' sugar

½ cup (1 stick) unsalted butter, at room temperature

¼ cup vegetable shortening

2 cups granulated sugar

1¼ cups heavy cream

½ cup (1 stick) unsalted butter, cut into pieces and chilled

4 cups chopped toasted walnuts or pecans

4 ounces semisweet chocolate, cut into pieces, or semisweet chocolate chips

UTENSILS NEEDED: Mixing bowl; pastry cutter; 13 × 9 × 2-inch baking pan, lightly buttered; heavy-bottomed saucepan; wooden spoon; spatula; small nonstick saucepan

BAKING TIME: Approximately 25 minutes

QUANTITY: Approximately 2 dozen

STORAGE: Keep airtight, individually wrapped, up to 1 week.

Combine the flour and confectioners' sugar in a mixing bowl. Add the room-temperature butter and vegetable shortening and, using a pastry cutter, work the fat into the dry ingredients to make a smooth dough. Scrape the dough from the bowl into the prepared pan and, using your fingertips, press out the dough to cover the bottom and come up the sides of the pan.

Bake for about 25 minutes, or until lightly browned and cooked through. Remove from the oven and set aside to cool to room temperature.

Place the granulated sugar in a heavy-bottomed saucepan over high heat. As soon as the sugar begins to melt, lower the heat and cook, stirring constantly with a wooden spoon, for about 5 minutes, or until the sugar turns into a thick, light brown syrup. Remove the pan from the heat and, stirring constantly, carefully and slowly pour ¾ cup of the heavy cream into the sugar syrup. The mixture will quickly foam and thicken. Immediately begin stirring the chilled butter, one piece at a time, into the hot mixture. When all of the butter is incorporated, you should have a thick syrup. Stir in the nuts and then pour the toffee mixture over the cooled crust, spreading it evenly with a spatula. Set aside to cool.

Combine the chocolate with the remaining ½ cup heavy cream in a small nonstick saucepan over medium heat. Cook, beating constantly, for about 3 minutes, or until the chocolate is melted into the cream. Immediately drizzle the liquid chocolate over the top of the set toffee to make a lacy, abstract pattern. Set aside to allow the chocolate to harden.

When the chocolate is set, cut the cookies into bars or squares.

Chubbies

PREHEAT OVEN TO: 350°F

UTENSILS NEEDED: Sifter; mixing bowl; electric mixer; at least 2 cookie sheets,
preferably nonstick, lightly buttered; wire racks

BAKING TIME: Approximately 12 minutes

QUANTITY: Approximately 3 dozen

STORAGE: Keep airtight, in layers separated by waxed or parchment paper, up to 1 week.

INGREDIENTS

- 2¼ cups sifted all-purpose flour
- ¼ cup Dutch-process cocoa powder
- 1 teaspoon baking soda
- ¾ cup (1½ sticks) unsalted butter, at room temperature
- ½ cup light brown sugar
- ½ cup granulated sugar
- 1 large egg
- 2 ounces unsweetened chocolate, melted and cooled
- ½ cup sour cream
- 2 teaspoons pure vanilla extract
- 1 cup semisweet chocolate chunks
- ¾ cup toasted macadamia nuts
- ½ cup toffee candy pieces, such as Heath Bars

Sift together the flour, cocoa powder, and baking soda into a mixing bowl. Set aside.

Place the butter in the bowl of an electric mixer and beat until creamy. Add the light brown and granulated sugars and egg and beat until light and fluffy. Beat in the melted chocolate, sour cream, and vanilla. Mix in the dry ingredients, about ½ cup at a time, beating well after each addition. When the batter is thoroughly mixed, stir in the chocolate chunks, macadamia nuts, and toffee candy pieces.

Drop the dough by the heaping tablespoonful onto the prepared cookie sheets, leaving about 1½ inches between each cookie. Bake for approximately 12 minutes, or until lightly browned at the edges and set in the center.

Remove from the oven and cool on wire racks before serving or storing.

Carrot Drops

PREHEAT OVEN TO: 350°F

INGREDIENTS

3 cooked carrots, chopped

¼ cup dark molasses

1½ teaspoons ground
   ginger

1 teaspoon ground
   cinnamon

½ teaspoon ground
   nutmeg

½ teaspoon baking soda

2 cups all-purpose flour

1 cup dried cranberries,
   cherries, or golden
   seedless raisins

UTENSILS NEEDED: Food processor; mixing bowl; wooden spoon; at least 2 cookie sheets, preferably nonstick, lightly buttered; wire racks

BAKING TIME: Approximately 12 minutes

QUANTITY: Approximately 2½ dozen

STORAGE: Keep airtight, in layers separated by waxed or parchment paper, up to 1 week.

Place the carrots in the bowl of a food processor fitted with the metal blade. Process to a smooth purée. Measure out 1 full cup and place it in a mixing bowl. Reserve the remaining purée, if any, for another use.

Add the molasses, ginger, cinnamon, nutmeg, and baking soda to the carrot purée. When well blended, beat in the flour with a wooden spoon. Fold in the cranberries.

Drop by the teaspoonful onto the prepared cookie sheets, leaving about 1½ inches between each cookie. Bake for about 12 minutes, or until the cookies are light brown around the edges and set in the center.

Remove from the oven and cool on wire racks before serving or storing.

Coconut Meringue Cookies

PREHEAT OVEN TO: 275°F

UTENSILS NEEDED: Electric mixer; at least 2 nonstick cookie sheets lined with
parchment paper; wire racks

BAKING TIME: Approximately 1 hour

QUANTITY: Approximately 4 dozen

STORAGE: Keep airtight, in layers separated by waxed or parchment paper, up to 3 days.
Do not freeze.

INGREDIENTS

4 large egg whites

1 cup superfine sugar

1 teaspoon cream of tartar

1 cup grated fresh coconut, toasted

Place the egg whites in the bowl of an electric mixer fitted with the wire whisk. Begin beating on slow and, when frothy, add ½ cup of the sugar and the cream of tartar and gradually increase the speed. As the egg whites stiffen, gradually add the remaining ½ cup sugar. When very stiff but not dry, fold in the coconut, taking care to distribute it evenly throughout the meringue.

Drop the meringue by the rounded teaspoonful onto the prepared cookie sheets, leaving about ½ inch between each cookie. Use the end of the teaspoon to lift the meringue in the center of each cookie, forming a little tip. (Alternatively, you can fill a large pastry bag fitted with a large, fluted tip with the meringue batter and pipe cookies onto the prepared sheets.) Bake for about 1 hour, or until the meringues are crisp and very lightly tinged with color. Do not allow the meringues to get too brown.

Remove from the oven and place on wire racks to cool completely before serving or storing.

NOTE: Meringues are best made when the ambient temperature is cool and dry, as hot, damp conditions will keep the meringues from drying out.

Chocolate Butter Balls

INGREDIENTS

2 cups sifted all-purpose
   flour

2 teaspoons baking
   powder

½ teaspoon salt

4 ounces unsweetened
   chocolate

½ cup unsalted butter, at
   room temperature

1½ cups granulated sugar

2 teaspoons pure vanilla
   extract

4 large eggs

½ cup finely chopped
   toasted pecans

Approximately 3 cups
   confectioners' sugar

PREHEAT OVEN TO: 375°F

UTENSILS NEEDED: Medium bowl; double boiler; electric mixer; shallow bowl or platter;
at least 2 cookie sheets, preferably nonstick, lightly buttered; wire racks

BAKING TIME: Approximately 12 minutes

QUANTITY: About 4 dozen

STORAGE: Layer between waxed or parchment paper and keep in an airtight container,
up to 2 weeks

———————————

Sift together the flour, baking powder, and salt in a medium bowl. Set aside.

Place the chocolate in the top half of a double boiler over very hot water. Stir until the chocolate is melted. Remove from the heat and allow to cool.

Place the butter in the bowl of an electric mixer and beat until creamy. Add the granulated sugar and vanilla and beat until light and fluffy. Add the eggs, one at a time, beating well after each addition. Beat in the cooled chocolate. When well mixed, add the dry ingredients and beat until combined. Stir in the pecans, taking care to distribute them evenly. Cover and refrigerate for about 30 minutes, or until chilled.

Place the confectioners' sugar in a large shallow bowl or platter.

When the dough is chilled, use your fingers to scoop up a small amount and roll it into a 1-inch ball. Roll the ball in confectioners' sugar and then place it on the prepared cookie sheet. Continue rolling and coating balls, placing them about 2 inches apart on the cookie sheets, until you have used all of the dough. (If using only 2 cookie sheets, this will have to be done in batches.) Place in the preheated oven and bake for about 12 minutes, or until lightly colored.

Remove from the oven and allow to cool on the cookie sheets for 5 minutes. Then, place the butter balls on wire racks to cool before serving or storing.

Mexican Wedding Cakes

PREHEAT OVEN TO: 350°F

UTENSILS NEEDED: Wooden spoon; mixing bowl; at least 2 cookie sheets, preferably nonstick, lightly buttered; shallow bowl or platter; wire racks

BAKING TIME: Approximately 15 minutes

QUANTITY: Approximately 3 dozen

STORAGE: Keep airtight, individually wrapped, up to 4 days.

INGREDIENTS

1 cup (2 sticks) unsalted butter, melted

½ cup plus 2 cups confectioners' sugar

2 cups sifted all-purpose flour

2 cups finely chopped blanched almonds or peanuts

1 teaspoon ground cinnamon

2 teaspoons pure vanilla extract

3 tablespoons Dutch-process cocoa powder

Using a wooden spoon, combine the melted butter with ½ cup of the confectioners' sugar in a mixing bowl. Beat in the flour, nuts, cinnamon, and vanilla.

Make one cookie at a time by scooping up a bit of dough and, using your fingers, rolling it into a 1-inch ball. Place on a prepared cookie sheet, allowing about 1½ inches between each ball of dough. Bake for about 15 minutes, or until just golden.

Combine the remaining 2 cups confectioners' sugar with the cocoa powder in a large shallow bowl or platter.

Remove the cookies from the oven and, while still hot, carefully roll each cookie in the confectioners' sugar mixture. Place on wire racks to cool before serving or storing.

Jam Turnovers

INGREDIENTS

2 cups sifted all-purpose flour

8 ounces cream cheese, cut into cubes and chilled

1 cup (2 sticks) unsalted butter, cut into cubes and chilled

Approximately 2 cups fine-quality raspberry, cherry, blueberry, or other jam of choice

Wondra flour for forming

CHILLING TIME: At least 12 hours

PREHEAT OVEN TO: 400°F

UTENSILS NEEDED: Mixing bowl; pastry cutter; baking pans with sides or platters that will fit into your refrigerator; 2 cookie sheets, preferably nonstick; wire racks

BAKING TIME: Approximately 10 minutes

QUANTITY: Approximately 5 dozen

STORAGE: Refrigerate, loosely covered, up to 1 week.

Place the flour in a mixing bowl. Add the cream cheese and butter and, using a pastry cutter or your fingertips, work the fats into the flour to make a smooth dough. Form the dough into 1-inch balls and place, in a single layer, on either baking pans or a platter. Refrigerate for at least 12 hours or up to 2 days. (If desired, the cookies can be frozen after they are chilled.)

When ready to bake, lightly flour a clean, dry surface with Wondra flour. Working with one ball at a time, flatten the dough into a neat circle with the palm of your hand or the bottom of a glass. Spoon about ½ teaspoon jam into the center of the circle and then fold up the sides to completely enclose the jam and make a semicircle of dough. Press the edges closed with the tines of a fork.

Place the turnovers on the cookie sheets, leaving about ½ inch between each cookie. Bake, watching carefully, as the dough can quickly burn, for about 10 minutes, or until just barely golden.

Remove from the oven and place on wire racks to cool before serving or storing.

Chocolate Sablés

CHILLING TIME: At least 6 hours

PREHEAT OVEN TO: 350°F

UTENSILS NEEDED: Mixing bowl; sifter; electric mixer; at least 2 cookie sheets lined with parchment paper; wire racks

BAKING TIME: Approximately 10 minutes

QUANTITY: Approximately 2½ dozen

STORAGE: Layer between waxed or parchment paper and keep in an airtight container, up to 1 week.

INGREDIENTS

1½ cups all-purpose flour

⅓ cup Dutch-process cocoa powder, sifted

½ teaspoon baking soda

½ cup (1 stick) unsalted butter, at room temperature

½ cup superfine sugar

1 large egg, at room temperature

1 teaspoon pure vanilla extract

¾ cup mini semisweet chocolate chips

Combine the flour, cocoa powder, and baking soda in a mixing bowl and sift them together two times.

Place the butter in the bowl of an electric mixer and beat until creamy. Add the sugar and continue to beat until light and fluffy. With the motor running, add the egg and then the vanilla, beating until the mixture is almost satin smooth.

Add the sifted dry ingredients to the creamed mixture, beating to incorporate. Stir in the mini chips.

Scrape the dough from the bowl and form it into 2 logs, each about 1¾ inches in diameter. Wrap the rolls in plastic film and tightly turn the ends closed. Hit each roll against a countertop to make it square. Refrigerate for at least 6 hours.

When ready to bake, unwrap the logs and, using a serrated knife, cut them crosswise into ¼-inch-thick slices. Place the cookies about 1 inch apart on the prepared cookie sheets. Bake for about 10 minutes, or until the cookies have risen slightly, are firm to the touch, and are lightly browned around the edges.

Remove from the oven and place on wire racks to cool before serving or storing.

Scotch Shortbread

PREHEAT OVEN TO: 300°F

UTENSILS NEEDED: Electric mixer; at least 2 nonstick cookie sheets or two 9-inch cake or pie pans; cookie press; wire racks

BAKING TIME: 10 to 20 minutes

QUANTITY: Approximately 6 to 8 dozen with cookie press; eighteen 1-inch wedges in cake or pie pans

STORAGE: Layer between waxed or parchment paper and keep in an airtight container, up to 1 week at room temperature or refrigerated up to 2 weeks.

INGREDIENTS

2 cups (4 sticks) unsalted butter, at room temperature (see Note, opposite)

1 cup superfine sugar

4⅓ cups sifted all-purpose flour

Silver dragees, glazed cherries or fruit pieces, colored sugar, or other decorative candies, optional

Place the butter in the bowl of an electric mixer and beat until creamy. Add the sugar and beat until the sugar is dissolved and the mixture is very light. Begin adding the flour, 1 cup at a time, beating well after each addition. Continue adding flour until a fairly firm dough is achieved. If the dough seems too soft, refrigerate for 20 minutes.

Place the dough in a cookie press fitted with a decorative disk and press the cookies onto the cookie sheets, at least ½ inch apart. Alternatively, press the dough into the cake or pie pans, using your fingertips to smooth the top and press the sides into the edge of the pan; prick the dough with a fork. If you wish, you can decorate the cookies with silver dragees, glazed fruit, colored sugar, or decorative candies. Bake for 10 to 20 minutes, or until just barely golden around the edges. Check frequently, as the rich dough will quickly darken and, if it does, the cookies are inedible.

Remove from the oven and place the cookies on wire racks to cool before serving or storing. If you baked the shortbread in the cake or pie pans, use a small serrated knife to cut it into wedges immediately upon removing it from the oven. Allow the wedges to cool in the pan before serving or storing.

NOTE: Because the only flavor in these cookies is from the butter, it is important to use very fresh premium butter.

Scotch Shortbread can be reinvented as a cocktail snack by cutting the sugar in half and adding 2 teaspoons curry powder, 1 teaspoon salt, ½ teaspoon ground cumin, and ½ teaspoon (or to taste) cayenne pepper. Use a cookie press to make small logs or decorative biscuits. Serve warm with cocktails.

Lemon Logs

PREHEAT OVEN TO: 400°F

UTENSILS NEEDED: Electric mixer; at least 2 cookie sheets, preferably nonstick, lightly buttered; cookie press fitted with the smallest circular tip; wire racks

BAKING TIME: Approximately 7 minutes

QUANTITY: Approximately 4 dozen

STORAGE: Layer between waxed or parchment paper and keep in an airtight container, up to 2 weeks.

INGREDIENTS

½ cup (1 stick) unsalted butter, at room temperature

½ cup sugar

4 large egg whites

1 cup sifted all-purpose flour

1 teaspoon lemon extract

1 teaspoon freshly grated lemon zest

Place the butter in the bowl of an electric mixer and beat until creamy. Add the sugar and continue beating until well blended. Add the egg whites, one at a time, beating well after each addition. Beat in the flour, then the lemon extract and lemon zest.

Place the dough into the cookie press. Press the cookies onto the prepared cookie sheets in 3- to 4-inch strips and at least 1½ inches apart. Bake for about 7 minutes, or until just lightly browned.

Remove from the oven and place on wire racks to cool before serving or storing.

Blackouts

INGREDIENTS

1 cup (2 sticks) unsalted butter, at room temperature

¾ cup superfine sugar

1 cup finely ground black walnuts (or other strongly flavored nut)

2 cups sifted all-purpose flour

1½ cups confectioners' sugar

2 tablespoons Dutch-process cocoa powder

UTENSILS NEEDED: Electric mixer; sifter; small round cookie cutter; rolling pin; at least 2 cookie sheets, preferably nonstick, lightly buttered; wire racks

BAKING TIME: Approximately 15 minutes

QUANTITY: Approximately 5 dozen

STORAGE: Keep in an airtight container, up to 10 days.

_____

Place the butter in the bowl of an electric mixer and beat until creamy. Add the superfine sugar and continue beating until airy and very pale. Stir in the nuts, making certain they are evenly distributed.

Place the flour in a sifter and gradually sift it into the creamed mixture as you stir, adding just enough to make a soft dough.

Sift together the confectioners' sugar and cocoa powder. Lightly coat a clean, flat surface with the mixture.

Transfer the dough to the sugared surface and lightly press it out with the palm of your hand. Cover the top with plastic film and, using a rolling pin, roll out the dough until it is ¼ inch thick.

Remove the plastic film and lightly dust the top of the dough with the sugar mixture. Cut the dough into small circles with a small cookie or biscuit cutter (no larger than 2 inches in diameter). Place the cookies on the prepared cookie sheet at least ½ inch apart. Bake for about 15 minutes, or until lightly browned.

Remove from the oven and let cool on the cookie sheets for 5 minutes. Transfer to sheets of waxed paper and again dust with the sugar mixture. Transfer to wire racks and allow to cool before serving or storing.

Wine Stars

CHILLING TIME: 3 hours

PREHEAT OVEN TO: 400°F

UTENSILS NEEDED: Sifter; electric mixer; at least 2 cookie sheets, preferably nonstick, lightly buttered; rolling pin; 2-inch star-shaped cookie cutter; wire racks

BAKING TIME: Approximately 10 minutes

QUANTITY: Approximately 6 dozen

STORAGE: Wrap individually in plastic film, loosely covered, and keep up to 1 week.

INGREDIENTS

3 cups sifted all-purpose flour

¾ teaspoon Chinese five-spice powder

½ teaspoon baking soda

½ cup (1 stick) unsalted butter, at room temperature

1⅓ cups light brown sugar

1 large egg, at room temperature

½ cup finely ground blanched almonds

2 tablespoons sherry wine

¼ teaspoon almond extract

Combine the sifted flour, five-spice powder, and baking soda, and then sift them together twice. Set aside.

Combine the butter and sugar in the bowl of an electric mixer and beat until light and fluffy. Beat in the egg and, when well combined, stir in the almonds. Stir in the sherry and almond extract.

Gradually add the dry ingredients to the creamed mixture, beating to blend well. Scrape down the bowl, cover, and refrigerate for 3 hours to chill well.

Lightly flour a clean, flat surface. Place half of the dough on the floured surface and lightly press it out with the palm of your hand. Cover the top with plastic film and, using a rolling pin, roll out the dough to ¼ inch thick.

Remove the plastic film and cut out the dough with the star cookie cutter. Place the cookies on the prepared cookie sheets at least ½ inch apart. Bake for about 10 minutes, or until lightly browned around the edges.

Continue making cookies as above with the remaining half of the dough.

When done, remove the cookies from the oven and place on wire racks to cool before serving or storing.

3

BREADS

OF ALL OF THE BAKING I DO, I MOST ENJOY MAKING BREAD. Once a week, I still make six to eight loaves of Low-Fat Yogurt Bread. One loaf is quickly demolished, a couple are refrigerated for toast and snacks, and the rest are frozen for later in the week or for house gifts (usually with a jar of jam). It is so unexpected that, for most people, a loaf of homemade bread is a treasured gift.

All of the breads in this section are relatively easy to prepare. I know that many cooks, even very good ones, panic at the thought of making bread–but not to worry. Although I do believe that the more you make bread, the easier it becomes, it is best just to dive right in and test the bread-baking waters; very, very rarely will that first loaf or two be inedible. Many heavy-duty mixers come with dough hooks so you no longer have to knead by hand, but I have to admit that kneading is my favorite part of bread making.

Yeast breads can, for the most part, be made in loaf pans, shaped in baskets, or baked free-form. I have given proper baking directions for each bread in this section but, once you get the hang of it, you can choose your favorite baking method. I like to form my breads by hand and bake them on a baking stone that has been sprinkled with a little cornmeal. Fruit and tea breads are best made in small loaf pans; I prefer 6 × 3-inch pans, probably because I inherited about four dozen of them from my mom. You can also purchase many types of disposable aluminum pans for bread baking.

Baking either yeast or quick breads requires you to follow a few rules. With yeast breads, one of the most common errors is dissolving the yeast in water that is either too hot or too cold. Rapid-Rise and other instant yeasts resolve the problem somewhat, but I find that whatever liquid is used in the bread should still be the proper temperature (105°–115°F for dry yeast and 85°F for compressed yeast). All other ingredients should be at room temperature. Yeast breads should be kneaded until they are almost satin smooth, and quick breads should be mixed until just blended, as overmixing will toughen the batter.

Homemade bread is one of life's great rewards and, given as a gift, it seems to perfectly express a cook's appreciation of friendship. It is always so welcome that it can be packed simply—particularly if it is still warm. Breadbaskets or boards, bread knives, and homemade butters and jams are terrific gifts to add to a loaf or two of homemade bread, and if the package is pulled together with a pretty kitchen towel, so much the better. When giving a specialty bread such as English Muffins (page 59), Date-Nut Bread (page 62), or Flour Tortillas (page 66), it is always nice to add a traditional accompaniment to the gift.

Semolina Bread

RISING TIME: Approximately 2 hours

PREHEAT OVEN TO: 425°F

UTENSILS NEEDED: Heavy-duty electric mixer fitted with the dough hook; large bowl, lightly coated with olive oil; clean kitchen towel; baking sheet, lightly oiled, or baking stone; small knife; wire racks

BAKING TIME: Approximately 30 minutes

QUANTITY: 2 loaves

STORAGE: Wrap tightly and keep at room temperature up to 3 days; refrigerated, up to 10 days; frozen, up to 6 months.

Combine the semolina and bread flours in the bowl of a heavy-duty electric mixer fitted with the dough hook. Stir in the yeast, salt, and sugar.

Combine the water and olive oil and, with the motor running, begin adding the liquid to the dry ingredients. Knead the dough on medium speed for about 10 minutes, or until smooth. Add the raisins and anise seeds and knead to just incorporate. Scrape the dough from the mixer bowl into the oiled bowl. Turn to coat all of the dough with oil. Cover and let rise for about 2 hours, or until almost tripled in size.

Lift the dough from the bowl and punch it down.

Lightly flour a clean, dry surface with Wondra flour. Place the dough on the floured surface and divide it in half. Knead each half by hand for a couple of minutes. Form each piece into a smooth, slightly flattened ball.

Place the dough balls on the prepared baking sheet or baking stone. Using a small, sharp knife, make slashes across the top of the dough. Bake for about 30 minutes, or until golden brown and crisp. Remove from the oven and place on wire racks to cool before serving or storing.

INGREDIENTS

2⅔ cups fine semolina flour

2 cups bread flour

2 (¾-ounce) packages instant-rise yeast

1 tablespoon coarse salt

1 tablespoon sugar

1¾ cups warm (115°F) water

1½ tablespoons extra-virgin olive oil

1½ cups golden seedless raisins

¼ cup toasted anise seeds

Wondra flour

Low-Fat Yogurt Bread

INGREDIENTS

12 cups white bread flour

*2 cups white wheat flour
(see Note, opposite)*

*1 cup coarsely ground
yellow cornmeal*

*3 (¾-ounce) packages
instant-rise yeast*

¾ cup sugar

1 tablespoon sea salt

2½ cups nonfat milk

2 cups nonfat plain yogurt

RISING TIME: 1½ hours

PREHEAT OVEN TO: 375°F

UTENSILS NEEDED: Large mixing bowl; medium saucepan; whisk; instant-read thermometer; wooden spoon; lightly buttered large mixing bowl; clean kitchen towel; pastry scraper; 2 baking stones or 2 heavy-duty baking sheets sprinkled with fine yellow cornmeal; wire racks

BAKING TIME: Approximately 35 minutes

QUANTITY: Approximately 6 loaves

STORAGE: Wrap tightly or place in resealable plastic bags. Keep at room temperature up to 3 days; refrigerated, up to 10 days; frozen, up to 6 months.

Combine the bread flour, white wheat flour, cornmeal, yeast, sugar, and salt in a large mixing bowl.

Heat the milk in a medium saucepan over medium heat. When just hot, remove from the heat and whisk in the yogurt. Measure the temperature with a thermometer; it should be no hotter than 115°F. If it is, set aside until the proper temperature is reached.

Stirring constantly with a wooden spoon, pour the warm milk mixture over the dry ingredients and beat to begin blending. When the dough gets too heavy to mix with the spoon, scrape it onto a lightly floured surface and begin kneading. Knead for about 12 minutes, or until the dough is well blended but still a bit tacky. This will not be a smooth, shiny bread dough. Scrape the dough into the buttered bowl, cover with a clean kitchen towel, and set aside in a warm spot to rise for about 1½ hours, or until doubled in size (see Note).

Uncover the dough and again place it on a lightly floured surface. Punch it down to release all of the air and knead for about 4 minutes.

Using a pastry scraper, cut the dough into at least 6 equal pieces (see Note). Form each piece into a loaf shape and place the loaves on the prepared stones or baking sheets. Bake for about 35 minutes, or until golden brown.

Remove from the oven and place on wire racks to cool before serving or storing.

NOTE: White wheat flour is available in some specialty food stores and supermarkets and from the Baker's Catalogue (see Resources, page 170).

You do not have to let this dough rise. You can knead and immediately form it into loaves and bake it. I choose to give it one rise to ensure that it is very tender.

This recipe makes a lot of dough from which you can make loaves of any size and any shape you desire (adjust baking times accordingly). It will, minimally, make 6 large loaves. You can bake the bread in loaf pans as well as free-form.

Spicy Breadsticks

RISING TIME: About 45 minutes

PREHEAT OVEN TO: 375°F

UTENSILS NEEDED: Heavy-duty food processor fitted with the plastic blade;
instant-read thermometer (optional); lightly buttered mixing bowl;
clean kitchen towel; rolling pin; 2 cookie sheets, preferably nonstick,
lightly dusted with fine cornmeal or semolina flour; wire racks

BAKING TIME: Approximately 12 minutes

QUANTITY: Approximately 2 dozen

STORAGE: Keep in an airtight container, up to 2 weeks.

INGREDIENTS

1 (¾-ounce) package
instant-rise yeast

3½ cups sifted bread flour

1 tablespoon sugar

1½ teaspoons sea salt

1¼ cups warm (115°F)
water

2 tablespoons extra-virgin
olive oil

1 cup freshly grated
Parmesan cheese

2 tablespoons cracked
black pepper

Place the yeast, flour, sugar, and salt in the bowl of a heavy-duty food processor fitted with the plastic blade. With the motor running, add the water (check the temperature with the thermometer) and olive oil. Process to incorporate. Add the cheese and pepper and continue to process to make a smooth dough.

Scrape the dough from the processor bowl into the buttered mixing bowl. Cover with a clean kitchen towel and set aside in a warm spot for about 45 minutes, or until doubled in size.

Scrape the dough from the bowl onto a lightly floured surface and, using the palms of your hands, spread the dough as much as you can. Cover with plastic film and, using a rolling pin, roll the dough out to a large (about 12 × 8-inch) rectangle. Cut the rectangle in half, lengthwise, to make two pieces of equal size.

Cut each rectangle into 12 strips. One at a time, roll each strip between the palms of your hands to make a rope of dough about 12 inches long and ⅓ inch thick. Place the dough ropes on the prepared cookie sheets at least ½ inch apart. Bake for about 12 minutes, or until light brown.

Carefully remove the breadsticks from the cookie sheets and place on wire racks to cool before serving or storing.

English Muffins

RISING TIME: Approximately 3 hours total

PREHEAT OVEN TO: 400°F

UTENSILS NEEDED: Instant-read thermometer; small mixing bowl; heavy-duty electric mixer
fitted with the dough hook; large mixing bowl, lightly buttered; clean, damp kitchen towel;
3-inch muffin rings, buttered (see Note); 1 baking sheet, lightly greased and dusted
with fine cornmeal; wire rack

BAKING TIME: Approximately 20 minutes

QUANTITY: 8 muffins

STORAGE: Refrigerate in an airtight container, up to 1 week. Alternatively, freeze up to 6 weeks.

INGREDIENTS

1 package (2½ teaspoons)
active dry yeast

½ cup warm (115°F) water

2 teaspoons honey

3¼ cups all-purpose flour

2 teaspoons sea salt

¾ cup warm (115°F) milk

1 large egg, at room
temperature

Combine the yeast with the warm water (check the temperature with the thermometer) and honey in a small mixing bowl. Stir to break up the yeast and set aside for 8 minutes, or until bubbling.

Combine the flour and sea salt in the bowl of a heavy-duty electric mixer fitted with the dough hook. Add the yeast mixture and beat to blend. Add the milk and egg, beating to knead to a smooth dough. If more liquid is required, add warm water, 1 teaspoon at a time.

Scrape the dough into the buttered mixing bowl. Cover with a clean, damp kitchen towel and set aside for about 2 hours, or until doubled in size.

Punch down the dough and then transfer it to a lightly floured flat surface. Knead by hand for 3 minutes. Cover with the damp kitchen towel and let rest for 30 minutes.

Place the muffin rings on the prepared baking sheet. Divide the dough into 8 equal pieces. Fit 1 piece into each muffin ring, pushing with your fingertips to flatten slightly. Again, cover with the damp kitchen towel and let rest for 30 minutes. Bake for 20 minutes, or until the muffins are golden and airy when pushed on the top. Remove from the oven and remove the rings. Transfer to a wire rack to cool before serving or storing.

NOTE: If you don't have muffin rings, clean tuna fish cans with both ends removed work very well; also, you can shape the muffins by hand. Muffins can also be cooked on a griddle on the stovetop, either in the rings or free-form, over medium-low heat for about 10 minutes per side.

Carrot-Ginger Tea Bread

INGREDIENTS

*2 large eggs, at room
  temperature*

¾ cup canola oil

*½ cup (about 10) puréed
  cooked prunes*

*1 cup freshly grated
  carrots*

*2 tablespoons minced
  candied or crystallized
  ginger*

*1 tablespoon ginger juice
  (see page 20)*

*2 teaspoons freshly grated
  orange zest*

1½ cups all-purpose flour

1 cup bran flour

1 cup light brown sugar

*2 teaspoons baking
  powder*

1 teaspoon baking soda

PREHEAT OVEN TO: 375°F

UTENSILS NEEDED: Mixing bowl; whisk; wooden spoon; large bowl; three 6-inch loaf
pans, lightly buttered and dusted with Wondra flour; wire rack

BAKING TIME: Approximately 25 minutes

QUANTITY: Three 6-inch loaves

STORAGE: Wrap tightly. Keep at room temperature up to 1 day; refrigerated,
up to 1 week; frozen, up to 3 months.

———————————

Place the eggs in a medium mixing bowl and whisk until frothy. Beat in the oil and prune purée. When well blended, using a wooden spoon, beat in the carrots, minced ginger, ginger juice, and orange zest.

Combine the all-purpose flour with the bran flour, brown sugar, baking powder, and baking soda in a large bowl. When blended, add the carrot mixture, beating with a wooden spoon to incorporate.

Spoon the batter into the prepared pans. Bake for about 25 minutes, or until the edges begin to pull away from the pans and a cake tester inserted into the center comes out clean.

Remove from the oven and invert onto a wire rack. Allow to cool before serving or storing.

Zucchini-Mustard Tea Bread

PREHEAT OVEN TO: 350°F

UTENSILS NEEDED: Food processor fitted with the metal blade; fine-mesh sieve; mixing bowls; wooden spoon; two 9-inch loaf pans or four 6-inch loaf pans, lightly buttered and dusted with Wondra flour; wire racks

BAKING TIME: Approximately 50 minutes

QUANTITY: Two 9-inch loaves or four 6-inch loaves

STORAGE: Wrap tightly. Keep at room temperature up to 2 days; refrigerated, up to 10 days; frozen, up to 6 months.

INGREDIENTS

Approximately 1 pound zucchini, washed, trimmed, and patted dry

2 cups all-purpose flour

2 teaspoons ground cinnamon

2 teaspoons baking soda

½ teaspoon baking powder

¼ teaspoon ground ginger

3 large eggs, at room temperature

1 cup granulated sugar

½ cup light brown sugar

¾ cup canola oil

1 cup finely chopped pecans

2 tablespoons mustard seeds

Chop the zucchini in a food processor fitted with the metal blade. Transfer to a fine-mesh sieve and place over a bowl to drain for 1 hour. Press against the squash to push out excess liquid.

Combine the flour with the cinnamon, baking soda, baking powder, and ginger and sift them together. Set aside.

Place the eggs in a mixing bowl and whisk them until very frothy. Add the granulated and brown sugars and, using a wooden spoon, beat to blend. Stir in the oil, then the pecans and mustard seeds.

Beat the dry ingredients into the egg mixture, stirring until very well combined. Pour the batter into the prepared pans. Bake for about 50 minutes, or until the edges begin to pull away from the pans and the tops are lightly browned.

Remove from the oven and invert onto wire racks. Turn the loaves top-side up and let cool before serving or storing.

Date-Nut Bread

PREHEAT OVEN TO: 325°F

UTENSILS NEEDED: Heatproof mixing bowl; wooden spoon; sifter; six 6-inch loaf pans or three 9-inch loaf pans, lightly buttered and dusted with Wondra flour; wire racks

BAKING TIME: 40 minutes total

QUANTITY: Six 6-inch loaves or three 9-inch loaves

STORAGE: Wrap tightly. Keep at room temperature up to 3 days; refrigerated, up to 10 days; frozen, up to 3 months.

INGREDIENTS

2 pounds whole pitted dates

2 teaspoons baking soda

2½ cups boiling water

3 tablespoons unsalted butter

1½ cups sugar

2 large eggs, lightly beaten, at room temperature

1 teaspoon pure vanilla extract

4 cups sifted all-purpose flour

3 cups large walnut pieces

Place the dates in a heatproof mixing bowl. Sprinkle the baking soda over the dates and then pour in the boiling water. Add the butter and, using a wooden spoon, stir until melted. Stir in the sugar and beat until it begins to dissolve. Beating constantly, add the eggs and then the vanilla.

Place the flour into a sifter and gradually sift it into the date mixture, incorporating it well after each addition. Stir in the walnut pieces.

Pour the batter into the prepared pans. Bake for 10 minutes. Raise the oven temperature to 350°F and continue to bake for an additional 30 minutes, or until a cake tester inserted into the center comes out clean.

Remove from the oven and invert onto wire racks. Turn the loaves top-side up and allow to cool before serving or storing.

Streusel Apple Bread

PREHEAT OVEN TO: 350°F

UTENSILS NEEDED: Mixing bowl; wooden spoon; a 9-inch round cake pan or two 6-inch loaf pans, lightly buttered and dusted with Wondra flour; wire rack

BAKING TIME: Approximately 25 minutes

QUANTITY: Two 6-inch loaves

STORAGE: Wrap tightly. Keep at room temperature 1 day; refrigerated, up to 5 days; frozen, up to 3 months.

INGREDIENTS

1½ cups plus 3 tablespoons all-purpose flour

2½ teaspoons ground cinnamon

2 teaspoons baking soda

½ teaspoon ground cloves

2½ cups peeled and finely chopped Granny Smith apples

¾ cup granulated sugar

⅓ cup plus 2 tablespoons Fat Replacement Fruit Purée (see page 27) or commercially prepared fat replacement such as Lighter Bake

1 large egg

1 large egg white

2 teaspoons pure vanilla extract

½ cup golden seedless raisins

¼ cup light brown sugar

Combine 1½ cups of the flour with 2 teaspoons of the cinnamon, the baking soda, and cloves. Set aside.

Combine the apples with the granulated sugar, ⅓ cup of the fat replacement purée, the whole egg, the egg white, and the vanilla. When well blended, stir in the raisins. Then, add the dry ingredients to the apple mixture, stirring just to incorporate. Set aside.

Combine the brown sugar with the remaining 3 tablespoons flour and ½ teaspoon cinnamon, mixing with your fingertips to blend. Using a fork, stir in the remaining 2 tablespoons fat replacement purée to make a crumbly mixture.

Pour the batter into the prepared pans. Sprinkle the streusel topping over each loaf. Bake for about 25 minutes, or until light brown.

Remove from the oven and place on a wire rack to cool before serving or storing.

Irish Soda Bread

RESTING TIME: 30 minutes

PREHEAT OVEN TO: 325°F

UTENSILS NEEDED: Sifter; heavy-duty mixer fitted with the dough hook;
medium bowl; whisk, pastry cutter; eight 8-inch loaf pans, lightly buttered and dusted
with Wondra flour; wire racks

BAKING TIME: Approximately 30 minutes

QUANTITY: Eight 8-inch loaves

STORAGE: Wrap tightly. Keep at room temperature 1 day; refrigerated, up to 5 days;
frozen, up to 6 months.

SERVING SUGGESTION: Best served warm. Cover with a damp cloth and reheat, at 300°F,
before serving

INGREDIENTS

8–10 cups all-purpose
flour

1½ cups sugar

⅓ cup baking powder

2 tablespoons ground
nutmeg

2 tablespoons ground
cinnamon

1½ cups golden seedless
raisins

5 large eggs, at room
temperature

1½ cups milk

Combine 8 cups of the flour with the sugar, baking powder, nutmeg, and cinnamon and sift together 3 times. Place in the bowl of a heavy-duty mixer fitted with the dough hook. Stir in the raisins.

In a separate bowl, whisk together the eggs and milk and, with the mixer running, beat the liquid into the dry ingredients, until doughy. If the dough seems sticky, add some additional flour, ½ cup at a time, just until a soft but kneadable dough forms.

Remove the bowl from the mixer and scrape down the sides. Cover and set aside to rest for 30 minutes.

Scrape the dough from the bowl and knead by hand for about 10 minutes, adding flour as necessary to keep the dough from sticking to your hands. Using a pastry cutter, divide the dough into 8 equal pieces. Fit a piece into each of the prepared pans, working with your fingers to smooth the top. Using a small, sharp knife, score the top of each loaf.

Bake for about 30 minutes, or until golden brown.

Remove from the oven and invert onto wire racks. Turn the loaves top-side up and allow to cool slightly before serving or cool entirely before storing. To reheat, cover with a damp cloth and warm at 300°F for about 15 minutes.

Spiced Real Corn Muffins

PREHEAT OVEN TO: 400°F

UTENSILS NEEDED: Mixing bowls; whisk;
wooden spoon; two 12-cup muffin tins,
lightly buttered; wire racks

BAKING TIME: Approximately 25 minutes

QUANTITY: 24 muffins

STORAGE: Keep in an airtight container,
at room temperature 1 day; refrigerated,
up to 3 days; frozen, up to 3 months.

Combine the flour, cornmeal, baking powder, sugar, black pepper, and salt in a mixing bowl.

Place the eggs in a small mixing bowl and whisk in the yogurt and milk. When well blended, whisk in the fat. With a wooden spoon, stir the liquid ingredients into the dry ingredients until just combined. Add the corn and jalapeño and stir to incorporate.

Spoon the batter into the buttered muffin cups; you should have enough batter to fill each ¾ full. Bake for about 25 minutes, or until golden brown.

Remove from the oven and serve or transfer to wire racks to cool before storing. Reheat before serving.

INGREDIENTS

2 cups all-purpose flour

2 cups coarsely ground (preferably stone-ground) cornmeal

1 tablespoon baking powder

1 tablespoon sugar

2 teaspoons cracked black pepper

1 teaspoon coarse salt, or to taste

2 large eggs

1 cup nonfat plain yogurt

½ cup milk

¾ cup melted unsalted butter, vegetable shortening, or bacon fat

1 cup cooked corn kernels

1 teaspoon minced jalapeño chile, or to taste

Flour Tortillas

4 cups all-purpose flour

1 teaspoon baking powder

1 teaspoon salt

¼ cup lard or vegetable shortening

2 cups hot water

Wondra flour

UTENSILS NEEDED: Sifter; electric mixer; rolling pin; cast-iron skillet, lightly greased; spatula; wire racks; waxed paper

COOKING TIME: Approximately 5 minutes

QUANTITY: Approximately 18 tortillas

STORAGE: Layer between waxed paper and keep in an airtight container, refrigerated, up to 3 days; frozen, up to 6 months.

Combine the flour, baking powder, and salt and sift them together twice into the bowl of an electric mixer. Cut the shortening into the dry ingredients. Slowly add the water, beating for about 10 minutes, or until the dough is very elastic.

Divide the dough into approximately 18 pieces, each about the size of a golf ball.

Lightly coat a clean, dry surface with Wondra flour. One piece at a time, place the dough on the floured surface and, using a rolling pin, roll out the dough to a circle about 8 inches in diameter. Using your hands, keep turning the dough to make a perfect circle.

Place the skillet over medium-high heat until it is very hot but not smoking. Cook the tortillas, one at a time, in the hot skillet for about 4 minutes, turning once, until light brown on both sides. Pat the dough down with the back of a spatula to keep bubbles from forming and popping. Grease the skillet as needed as you continue to cook the tortillas.

Serve warm, or place the cooked tortillas on wire racks to cool before storing. To reheat, wrap in aluminum foil and warm in a low oven.

Hola! Flour Tortillas

Nana's Doughnuts

INGREDIENTS

3½ cups all-purpose flour

1 tablespoon baking powder

½ teaspoon salt

½ teaspoon ground nutmeg

1½ cups granulated sugar

2 tablespoons unsalted butter, at room temperature

3 large eggs, beaten

½ cup milk

Wondra flour

Approximately 4 cups cinnamon sugar or confectioners' sugar, optional (see Note, opposite)

Approximately 6 cups vegetable oil

UTENSILS NEEDED: Sifter; electric mixer fitted with paddle; doughnut cutter; brown paper or resealable plastic bag; heavy-duty skillet, at least 3 inches deep; instant-read thermometer; slotted spoon; paper towel or newspaper; wire racks

HEAT VEGETABLE OIL TO: 360°F

FRYING TIME: Approximately 4 minutes

QUANTITY: Approximately 2 dozen

STORAGE: Keep in an airtight container at room temperature, up to 2 days (see Note).

Sift together the flour, baking powder, salt, and nutmeg. Set aside.

Place the granulated sugar and butter in the bowl of an electric mixer fitted with the paddle and beat until incorporated. Beat in the eggs and then the milk. Add the dry ingredients and beat until a smooth dough forms.

Lightly flour a clean, dry surface with Wondra flour. Scrape the dough onto the floured surface and lightly sprinkle Wondra flour over the top. Pat the dough out to about ⅝-inch thickness. (If dough is too sticky, knead about ¼ to ½ cup all-purpose flour into the dough.) Using a doughnut cutter, cut out doughnuts, reserving the holes separately.

If using, place about 4 cups cinnamon sugar or confectioners' sugar in a brown paper bag or resealable plastic bag. Set aside.

Place the skillet over medium-high heat. Add the vegetable oil and heat until it registers 360°F on an instant-read thermometer.

Place the doughnuts, a few at a time, in the hot oil and fry, turning once, for about 4 minutes, or until perfectly browned, slightly raised, and cooked through. Using a slotted spoon, move the doughnuts to a triple layer of paper towel or newspaper to drain for just a minute.

Quickly transfer the hot doughnuts to the sugar in the bag and shake to coat. Remove the sugar-coated doughnuts from the bag and place on wire racks to rest for a couple of minutes before eating warm.

Continue frying until all of the doughnuts are cooked. Fry the doughnut holes for about 2 minutes, or until perfectly browned, as above. Drain and coat as for doughnuts. Serve warm.

NOTE: Doughnuts are really best served hot from the pan. However, these old-fashioned favorites are so good that I often make them early in the morning and then take them along for a weekend morning's breakfast or brunch gift.

You can serve the doughnuts plain or coat them in any sugar or flavored sugar. Granulated sugar, confectioners' sugar, cinnamon sugar, cocoa sugar, and spiced sugar each make a great coating.

Scallion Pancakes

INGREDIENTS

2 large eggs

1 cup milk

½ cup all-purpose flour

¼ teaspoon salt, or to
taste

⅓ cup chopped scallions,
some green included

1 tablespoon toasted
sesame seeds

½ teaspoon Asian
sesame oil

¼ teaspoon chile oil,
or to taste

RESTING TIME: 30 minutes

UTENSILS NEEDED: Mixing bowl; whisk; 7-inch nonstick frying pan,
lightly coated with nonstick vegetable spray; spatula; warm plate

FRYING TIME: Approximately 1½ minutes

QUANTITY: Approximately 1 dozen

STORAGE: Keep uncovered, at room temperature, up to 4 hours. Alternatively,
cover tightly and refrigerate up to 3 days; or freeze, separated with waxed
or freezer paper, up to 3 months.

Combine the eggs and milk in a mixing bowl. Whisk in the flour and salt. When well blended, cover and set aside to rest for 30 minutes.

Whisk in the scallions, sesame seeds, and sesame and chile oils.

Heat the frying pan over medium-high heat. Ladle in about 3 tablespoons of the batter, swirling to coat the bottom of the pan. Cook for about 1 minute, or until golden around the edges. Carefully turn and fry the remaining side for about 30 seconds, or just until set. Using a spatula, transfer to a warm plate. Continue making pancakes, respraying the pan with nonstick vegetable spray, if necessary, until all of the batter is used.

Serve warm or store as directed. Reheat, uncovered, in a low oven.

Homemade Butter

UTENSILS NEEDED: Blender or food processor fitted with the plastic blade;
fine-mesh sieve; mixing bowl

QUANTITY: Approximately 1 cup

STORAGE: Keep in an airtight container and refrigerate, up to 1 week;
freeze, up to 3 months.

INGREDIENTS

1 cup ice-cold premium heavy (whipping) cream
2 large ice cubes, chopped
½ cup ice water
Sea salt to taste, optional

Place the cream in a blender or food processor fitted with the plastic blade. Cover and process at the highest speed for about 2 minutes, or until the cream is whipped. Uncover and add the chopped ice cubes and ice water. Cover and process at the highest speed for about 3 minutes, or until the whipped cream turns to very light yellow particles of butter.

Drain the mixture through a fine-mesh sieve. When completely drained of water, transfer to a small mixing bowl. To add salt, use a rubber spatula or wooden spoon to work the butter for about 4 minutes, or until smooth.

Scrape the butter from the bowl into a clean container with a cover, such as a butter crock.

FRUIT BUTTER: For every 1 cup butter, do not add salt but work in ¼ cup well-drained chopped fresh strawberries or raspberries or ¼ cup peach purée when smoothing the butter particles.

HERB BUTTER: For every 1 cup butter, add salt along with 3 tablespoons finely chopped fresh flat-leaf parsley, cilantro, or chives *or* 2 tablespoons finely chopped fresh basil, tarragon, sage, or thyme leaves when smoothing the butter particles.

SEASONED BUTTER: For every 1 cup butter, add salt and white pepper to taste along with 1 teaspoon minced garlic or shallots *or* 1 tablespoon freshly grated horseradish *or* 2 minced canned anchovy fillets *or* 1 teaspoon freshly grated ginger root when smoothing the butter particles.

LIQUEUR-SCENTED BUTTER: For every 1 cup butter, do not add salt but work in ½ cup confectioners' sugar and ½ teaspoon freshly grated orange or lemon zest, along with 3 tablespoons brandy, Grand Marnier, or rum when smoothing the butter particles.

4

CANDIES & NUTS

ALMOST NO ONE MAKES CANDY AT HOME ANYMORE, which makes it one of the most unexpected and appreciated gifts from the kitchen. Even during the years when I was not doing much cooking, I always made my famous fudge at Christmastime because people requested it. But so many types of candy are easily made at home that, in recent years, I've gone back to experimenting with candy making. The recipes I have gathered reflect both old-fashioned and contemporary tastes.

In the home kitchen, there are two basic methods of candy making, one requiring a candy thermometer and one that does not. The latter is usually quicker and easier and the one to try if you have never before made candy. However, whichever method you choose, I think you will find that candy making is much easier than you anticipated.

I am the original by-the-seat-of-the-pants cook, but even I follow instructions when making candy. You cannot substitute ingredients, so be sure to read the ingredients list carefully. You must use heavy-duty pans that properly diffuse the heat and a wooden spoon for stirring. If the recipe calls for a temperature reading, you must have a candy thermometer. (These are available in many types ranging from simple, inexpensive glass models to high-tech digital delights, none of which are terribly expensive. Any of them will make a nice addition to the kitchen.) Finally, for the most part, candies should be individually wrapped for storing. Other than these few particulars, it is best just to take a deep breath and give candy making a try. I'll guarantee that even with your first attempt you'll produce a tasty batch. The candy may not *look* as professional as you'd like, but it will sure *taste* good.

No matter what container you use, when packing candies for giving, always make sure they are packed so that they will be as attractive when opened as they were when packed. This might mean wrapping each piece individually in plastic film, placing each piece in a paper cup especially made for candy, or layering the candies in a tin, carefully separated by colorful papers. Candy is usually best packed for giving in tin, glass, or other solid containers that keep moisture out and freshness in. Because candy is such an unexpected homemade gift and most gift containers are reusable, your gift will seem especially extravagant.

Truffles

UTENSILS NEEDED: Mixing bowl; whisk; double boiler; 8-inch square cake pan, lined with aluminum foil

COOKING TIME: Approximately 7 minutes

COOLING TIME: 2 hours

QUANTITY: Approximately 2 pounds

STORAGE: Keep individually wrapped candies in an airtight container at room temperature up to 1 week; refrigerated, up to 3 weeks.

INGREDIENTS

1 large egg white

2 tablespoons brandy

1½ cups confectioners' sugar

1½ cups finely ground toasted almonds

2 tablespoons Dutch-process cocoa powder

1½ cups finely chopped fine-quality unsweetened chocolate

¾ cup sweetened condensed milk

1 tablespoon unsalted butter, at room temperature

Combine the egg white and brandy in a mixing bowl, whisking to blend. Add the sugar, almonds, and cocoa powder, stirring to combine. Knead the mixture together with your hands.

When blended, scrape the mixture into the prepared pan and, using your fingertips, spread out the mixture to a smooth, even layer.

Place the chocolate in the top half of a double boiler over simmering water. Cook, stirring constantly, until melted. Beat in the milk and butter and cook for about 7 minutes, or until thick. Immediately pour the chocolate mixture over the nut layer in the pan, spreading it out with a spatula to make a smooth, even layer.

Allow to cool for 2 hours. Cut into ¾-inch squares and serve or store.

My Never-Ever-Fail
Chocolate Fudge

INGREDIENTS

*12 ounces bittersweet or
semisweet chocolate,
finely chopped*

*2 cups toasted walnut,
pecan, macadamia,
or other nuts, chopped,
optional*

*10 tablespoons unsalted
butter, at room
temperature*

*1 tablespoon pure vanilla
extract*

20 large marshmallows

4 cups sugar

*2 5-ounce cans evaporated
milk*

UTENSILS NEEDED: Heatproof bowl; heavy-bottomed saucepan;
baking sheet or platter, lightly buttered; wooden spoon

BOILING TIME: 6 minutes

QUANTITY: Approximately 8 dozen pieces

STORAGE: Keep individually wrapped candies in an airtight
container at room temperature up to 1 week;
refrigerated, up to 3 weeks.

———————

Combine the chocolate pieces, nuts (if using), butter, and vanilla in a large heat-proof bowl. Set aside.

Place the marshmallows, sugar, and evaporated milk in a heavy-bottomed saucepan over medium heat. Stirring constantly, bring to a boil. Continuing to stir, boil for exactly 6 minutes.

Remove from the heat and immediately pour the marshmallow mixture into the chocolate mixture; beat constantly until creamy. Quickly pour into the pre-pared pan or platter, pushing slightly with the back of a wooden spoon to spread the fudge evenly.

Cool for at least 1 hour before cutting into pieces. Serve at room temperature.

Good-for-You Snack Bars

1 cup organic applesauce

2 cups natural grain puffed cereal

1¼ cups all-purpose flour

¾ cup light brown sugar

2 tablespoons soy milk powder or nonfat dry milk powder

3 tablespoons toasted wheat germ

1 teaspoon ground cinnamon

1 teaspoon baking soda

2 large egg whites

1 cup fresh blueberries, washed and dried

⅓ cup canola oil

½ cup dried blueberries, cherries, or cranberries

½ teaspoon pure vanilla extract

1 tablespoon flaxseed (see Note)

PREHEAT OVEN TO: 350°F

UTENSILS NEEDED: Fine-mesh sieve; cheesecloth; food processor fitted with the metal blade; 13 × 9 × 2-inch baking pan, lightly coated with nonstick vegetable spray; wire racks

BAKING TIME: Approximately 30 minutes

QUANTITY: Approximately 2 dozen

STORAGE: Keep individually wrapped bars in an airtight container at room temperature up to 1 week; refrigerated, up to 1 month.

Line a fine-mesh sieve with a double layer of cheesecloth. Add the applesauce and place over a bowl to drain for 30 minutes.

Place the cereal in the bowl of a food processor fitted with the metal blade and process for about 1 minute or until coarsely ground. Add the flour, brown sugar, dry milk powder, wheat germ, cinnamon, and baking soda and process to just blend.

Add the drained applesauce along with the egg whites, fresh blueberries, oil, dried berries, and vanilla, processing to just combine. Stir in the flaxseed.

Scrape the batter into the prepared pan. Bake for about 30 minutes, or until a cake tester inserted into the center comes out clean.

Remove from the oven and place the pan on a wire rack to cool. When cool, use a sharp knife to cut into bars or squares. Serve or individually wrap in plastic film before storing.

NOTE: Flaxseed is available at health food stores and some supermarkets.

Fruit Jellies

UTENSILS NEEDED: Heavy-bottomed nonstick saucepan; fine-mesh sieve; spatula; large bowl; wooden spoon; metal spoon for skimming; candy thermometer; 8-inch square cake pan, lightly coated with vegetable oil; shallow bowl; small, sharp knife

COOKING TIME: Approximately 30 minutes

SETTING TIME: 4 days

QUANTITY: Approximately 1½ pounds

STORAGE: Keep individually wrapped jellies in an airtight container in a cool spot up to 1 month.

INGREDIENTS

2 pounds raspberries, strawberries, or blueberries, washed and dried

3⅔ cups sugar

Place the berries in a heavy-bottomed nonstick saucepan over medium-low heat. Cover and cook for about 5 minutes, or until the berries are easily mashed.

Transfer the berries to a fine-mesh sieve and, using a spatula, press against the pulp to strain off the juice into a large bowl.

Wipe the saucepan clean and return the juice to it. Stir in 2⅔ cups of the sugar and place over medium-low heat. Cook, stirring constantly with a wooden spoon, until the sugar is dissolved. Bring to a gentle boil. Maintain the boil, stirring constantly and occasionally skimming off the foam that rises to the top with a metal spoon, for about 30 minutes, or until the mixture reaches 230°F on a candy thermometer and begins to come away from the edge of the pan.

Remove from the heat and pour into the prepared pan. Loosely cover and place in a cool, dry spot to set for 4 days.

Place the remaining 1 cup sugar in a shallow bowl. Set aside.

Using a small, sharp knife, cut into ¾-inch squares or use tiny hors d'oeuvre cutters to cut the jellies into fancy shapes. Roll each jelly in the sugar and serve or store.

Candied Grapefruit Peel

INGREDIENTS

5 large unblemished
    grapefruit, preferably
    organic, washed and
    dried

3 cups sugar

1 cup very hot water

⅓ cup light corn syrup

UTENSILS NEEDED: Small, sharp knife; saucepan; heavy-bottomed nonstick saucepan; candy thermometer; shallow bowl; tongs; wire racks

COOKING TIME: Approximately 70 minutes

RESTING TIME: 1 hour

QUANTITY: About ½ pound

STORAGE: Layer candies between waxed or parchment paper and keep in an airtight container up to 1 month.

———

Using a small, sharp knife, carefully remove the peel from the grapefruit in quarters. Scrape as much of the pulp and white membrane as possible from the peel. Cut each piece of the peel lengthwise into ¼-inch-wide strips.

Place the strips in a saucepan with cold water to cover by 1 inch over high heat. Bring to a boil, lower the heat, and simmer for 15 minutes.

Remove from the heat and drain well. Repeat the process and cook for another 15 minutes, or until the peel is very tender. Drain well and pat dry.

Trim off any remaining white membrane to leave thin strips of pure peel. Set aside.

Combine 2 cups of the sugar with the hot water and corn syrup in a heavy-bottomed nonstick saucepan and cook over medium-high heat. Stirring constantly, bring to a boil and maintain it just until the sugar is dissolved. Add the reserved peel and bring to a simmer. Simmer for about 40 minutes, or until the mixture reaches 236°F on a candy thermometer and the peel is almost transparent.

Place the remaining 1 cup sugar in a shallow bowl.

Remove the pot from the heat and, using tongs, lift the slices of peel from the syrup and place them in a single layer on wire racks to drain. When well drained, roll each piece of peel in the sugar until well coated. Return to the wire racks to rest for 1 hour before serving or storing.

Mole Brittle

UTENSILS NEEDED: Heavy-bottomed nonstick saucepan; candy thermometer; one 11 × 7 × 2-inch baking pan, lightly coated with vegetable oil; large, sharp knife or cleaver; wire racks

COOKING TIME: Approximately 45 minutes

COOLING TIME: 2 hours

SETTING TIME: 2 hours

QUANTITY: Approximately 4 pounds

STORAGE: Layer between waxed or parchment paper and keep in an airtight container in a cool, dry spot up to 1 month.

INGREDIENTS

4 cups sugar

1 cup light corn syrup

1 tablespoon pure chile powder (not commercially prepared chili powder)

4 cups roasted, unsalted, skinless peanuts (or other nuts)

½ cup sesame seeds

1 ounce unsweetened chocolate, melted

2½ teaspoons baking soda

1½ tablespoons unsalted butter, at room temperature

Combine the sugar and corn syrup in a heavy-bottomed nonstick large saucepan over medium heat. Add the chile powder and cook, stirring constantly, until the sugar is dissolved. Promptly hook the thermometer onto the edge of the pan, making sure it falls into the liquid but does not hit the edge of the pan. Cook the syrup, without stirring, for about 25 minutes, or until the mixture reaches 240°F on the candy thermometer. Immediately stir in the nuts and sesame seeds and continue cooking for an additional 15 minutes, or until the mixture reaches 300°F on the candy thermometer.

Remove from the heat and immediately add the chocolate, baking soda, and butter, stirring to combine. The mixture will foam, so work quickly and carefully. As soon as the ingredients are blended, pour the mixture into the prepared pan. Set aside to cool for 2 hours.

When cool, use a sharp knife or cleaver to break the candy into serving pieces. Pull the pieces apart and set aside on wire racks to rest for 2 hours before serving or storing.

Caramelized Almonds

INGREDIENTS

2¼ cups whole almonds (skin on)

1½ cups sugar

UTENSILS NEEDED: Heavy-bottomed nonstick saucepan; large bowl of ice; large soupspoon; baking sheet, lightly buttered

COOKING TIME: Approximately 15 minutes

COOLING TIME: 1 hour

QUANTITY: Approximately 3 dozen

STORAGE: Layer between waxed or parchment paper and keep in an airtight container up to 1 month (see Note).

Combine the almonds with the sugar in a heavy-bottomed nonstick saucepan over medium heat. Cook, stirring constantly, until the sugar is dissolved. Continue to cook, stirring constantly, for about 15 minutes, or until the sugar is deeply caramelized and slightly thick.

Immediately remove from the heat and quickly dip the pan into a bowl of ice to stop the cooking. Immediately remove the pan from the ice. Using a large soupspoon and working quickly, drop the mixture by the spoonful onto the prepared baking sheet. When all of the candies are made, set aside to cool for 1 hour before serving or storing.

NOTE: It is very important that these candies be kept in an airtight container or they will become soft and sticky—tasty still, but very messy!

Spiced Candied Nuts

PREHEAT OVEN TO: 350°F

UTENSILS NEEDED: 2 nonstick baking pans; mixing bowl; wooden spoon; tongs or a long fork

BAKING TIME: 15 minutes

QUANTITY: Approximately 4 cups

STORAGE: Layer between waxed or parchment paper and keep in an airtight container up to 1 month.

INGREDIENTS

5 cups unsalted mixed nuts

4 cups confectioners' sugar

2 large egg whites, lightly beaten

½ cup canola oil

1 tablespoon brandy or freshly squeezed orange juice

1 teaspoon ground cinnamon

1 teaspoon ground nutmeg

½ teaspoon ground cardamom

½ teaspoon Chinese five-spice powder

¼ teaspoon pure chile powder (not commercially prepared chili powder), or to taste

Place the nuts on one nonstick baking pan in the preheated oven and roast, turning occasionally, for 15 minutes, or until lightly toasted and very aromatic.

While the nuts are roasting, prepare the coating.

Place the confectioners' sugar in a mixing bowl. Add the egg whites, oil, and brandy and, using a wooden spoon, beat to combine. Stir in the cinnamon, nutmeg, cardamom, five-spice powder, and chile powder. Pour the hot nuts into the sugar mixture, stirring to combine.

Using tongs or a fork, lift the nuts, one at a time, from the sugar mixture and place on the remaining nonstick baking sheet to dry for 2 hours before serving or storing.

5

JELLIES, JAMS & MARMALADES

IMPORTED OR DOMESTIC, LOCALLY PRODUCED or regionally manufactured, jellies, jams, and marmalades have become common in the American pantry. The shelves of gourmet food shops and even supermarkets abound with fine, exotic sweet spreads. But no matter how superb or unusual the commercial product, it will never equal the ultimate—preserves made in a home kitchen.

The wide availability of a variety of fruits, vegetables, and herbs has now made it possible to prepare jams and jellies all year long, but I still prefer to preserve seasonally. Since I live in the East, summer is a busy time in my kitchen. I always make strawberry, blueberry, raspberry, and peach jam—even if just a small batch to get us through the year. I've done this for so long that my husband knows the routine and even helps pick and can the fruit.

Here are a few hints that will help make preserving an easy gift-giving task.

- Always plan in advance. Unless you have assembled a pantry full of canning pots, jars, lids, and pectin, preserving is not a spur-of-the-moment activity.

- Familiarize yourself with canning procedures.

- Make sure all equipment is clean and free of cracks, chips, and rust. Spoilage is often caused by unclean or damaged equipment.

- Keep your work area clean and uncluttered.

- Use the exact ingredients called for in a specific recipe.

- Make sure you have enough containers and lids.

- Measure out all the ingredients before beginning the recipe procedure.

- Keep all jars and lids in a hot, sterilizing bath until they are filled. Jars must be hot when filled.

- Fill and seal jars one at a time.

- Make sure all rims, lids, and edges are food-free before sealing.

- Label every jar with the contents and date.

- Above all, take your time!

Jellies, jams, and marmalades—indeed, any food with a high level of sugar or vinegar—can be preserved using the open-kettle method. In this simple method, the food to be preserved is cooked, brought to the boiling point, and immediately poured into hot, sterilized jars that are sealed with sterilized, rubber-edged lids and screw caps. Food preserved by the open-kettle method has a shelf life of approximately one year.

The general directions for open-kettle canning are as follows: Cook the food for the length of time specified in the recipe in an uncovered large pot. When the cooking is completed, pour the boiling-hot mixture into hot jars that have been boiled in water to cover for 5 minutes. Fill and seal one jar at a time. Wipe the sealing edge with a clean, dry cloth (a batch of damp paper towel works well). Place a hot, sterilized lid on the jar and cover with a screw top. Immediately turn the jar over to heat the lid.

Let the jars remain upside-down for 5 minutes and then set them right-side up, about 2 inches apart, on wire racks. Let cool. The jars are now vacuum-sealed. Label and store the jars in a cool, dry place.

Most jellies, jams, and marmalades can also be placed in attractive containers without creating a vacuum seal and stored in the refrigerator or freezer for shorter periods. However, to ensure bacteria-free preserving, you should still sterilize the containers and lids before packing. When refrigerating the hot-packed containers, place them in the coldest part of the refrigerator, leaving at least 1 inch on all sides to speed cooling.

The old-fashioned canning jar is a welcome gift container in itself. However, it is always fun to think of other ways to make an attractive package. I never spend too much time trimming the jars themselves, although if so inclined you can spend many artistic hours doing so. I usually wrap the jars in netting, useful sparkling-white kitchen towels, or pretty napkins. When I want to give a more elaborate gift, I might give a sampling of jams and jellies and add some Homemade Butter (see page 71), an antique jelly dish and spoon, or some bread, or I might even pack a bountiful gift basket with an assortment of all of these.

Cassis Jelly

UTENSILS NEEDED: Heavy-bottomed saucepan; for preserving, eight 4-ounce canning jars and lids, sterilized; for refrigerating, eight 4-ounce containers with lids, sterilized; metal spoon

COOKING TIME: 16 minutes

QUANTITY: Eight 4-ounce containers

STORAGE: Vacuum-sealed jars last 1 year; refrigerated, up to 6 weeks.

SERVING SUGGESTIONS: Use as garnish or glaze for roast poultry or game. Substitute for currant jelly in sauces, desserts, and glazes.

INGREDIENTS

3 cups currant juice or cranberry-apple juice, preferably organic (see Note)

1 cup crème de cassis

2 tablespoons freshly squeezed lemon juice, strained

3¼ cups sugar

1 3-ounce packet liquid pectin

Combine the juice, crème de cassis, lemon juice, and sugar in a heavy-bottomed saucepan and bring to a boil over high heat, stirring constantly. Add the pectin and cook, stirring constantly, for about 15 minutes, or until the mixture comes to a full, rolling boil. Continue to boil for 1 more minute.

Remove the saucepan from the heat and, using a metal spoon, skim off and discard any foam that rises to the top. Immediately pour the jelly into the sterilized jars, cover, and vacuum-seal as directed on page 86, or pour into containers, cover, and set aside to cool before refrigerating.

NOTE: Organic currant juice is available at most health food stores.

Parsley Jelly

UTENSILS NEEDED: Heatproof bowl; fine-mesh sieve; cheesecloth; bowl; heavy-bottomed saucepan; for preserving, six 4-ounce canning jars and lids, sterilized; for refrigerating, six 4-ounce containers with lids, sterilized

BOILING TIME: 1 minute

QUANTITY: Six 4-ounce containers

STORAGE: Vacuum-sealed jars last 1 year; refrigerated, up to 6 weeks.

SERVING SUGGESTION: Use as garnish or glaze for poultry, fish, veal, or lamb.

Place the parsley in a heatproof bowl. Add the boiling water, cover the bowl with plastic film, and let stand for 15 minutes.

Line a fine-mesh sieve with cheesecloth and pour the parsley and water through it into a clean bowl, pressing on the solids to extract all of the flavor.

Measure 3 cups of the parsley juice and place it in a heavy-bottomed saucepan. Stir in the pectin and lime juice and place over high heat. Stirring constantly, bring to a full, rolling boil, then stir in the sugar and food coloring. Again, stirring constantly, bring to a full, rolling boil and boil for 1 minute.

Remove from the heat and immediately pour the jelly into the sterilized jars, cover, and vacuum-seal as directed on page 86, or pour into containers, cover, and set aside to cool before refrigerating.

INGREDIENTS

4 cups chopped fresh parsley, preferably organic

3 cups boiling water

1 1.75-ounce packet powdered pectin

2 tablespoons freshly squeezed lime juice

4½ cups sugar

Few drops green food coloring

Hot Pepper Jelly

UTENSILS NEEDED: Food processor fitted with the metal blade; heavy-bottomed saucepan; for preserving, ten 4-ounce canning jars and lids, sterilized; for refrigerating, ten 4-ounce containers with lids, sterilized

BOILING TIME: 10 minutes

QUANTITY: Ten 4-ounce containers

STORAGE: Vacuum-sealed jars last 1 year; refrigerated, up to 3 months.

SERVING SUGGESTIONS: Use as a glaze for or an accompaniment to meats, game, or poultry or as an hors d'oeuvre with cream cheese on water crackers.

INGREDIENTS

2 medium yellow or green bell peppers (preferably organic), washed, cores, seeds, and membranes removed, and chopped

1 cup chopped organic jalapeño, serrano, bird, or other hot chiles, washed and stemmed (see Note)

1½ cups white vinegar

6½ cups sugar

2 3-ounce packets liquid pectin

1 tablespoon dried red pepper flakes

Few drops green food coloring, optional

Combine the bell peppers, chiles, and vinegar in the bowl of a food processor fitted with the metal blade and pulse until finely ground. Transfer the mixture to a heavy-bottomed saucepan.

Place over high heat and, while stirring constantly, add the sugar. Cook, stirring constantly, for about 20 minutes, or until the mixture comes to a full, rolling boil. Continue to boil for 10 minutes.

Remove from the heat and stir in the pectin, red pepper flakes, and, if using, the food coloring. Immediately pour the jelly into the sterilized jars, cover, and vacuum-seal as directed on page 86, or pour into containers, cover, and set aside to cool before refrigerating.

NOTE: If desired, remove the seeds from the chiles to lower the heat index.

Pure Fruit Jam

INGREDIENTS

4 cups peeled, pitted (or seeded), and chopped very ripe fresh fruit, preferably organic

1 cup peeled, pitted (or seeded), and chopped barely ripe fresh fruit, preferably organic

½ cup frozen organic apple juice concentrate, thawed

3 tablespoons organic white grape juice

2 tablespoons freshly squeezed lemon juice

1 teaspoon pure vanilla extract

4 ounces (¼ cup) liquid pectin

UTENSILS NEEDED: Heavy-bottomed nonstick saucepan; six 8-ounce canning jars and lids, sterilized

COOKING TIME: Approximately 25 minutes

QUANTITY: Six 8-ounce jars

STORAGE: Vacuum-sealed jars last 1 year.

Combine the fruit, apple juice concentrate, grape juice, lemon juice, and vanilla in a heavy-bottomed nonstick saucepan over high heat. Add the pectin and cook, stirring constantly, for about 20 minutes, or until the mixture comes to a full, rolling boil. Lower the heat and simmer, stirring constantly, for 5 minutes, or until slightly thick. Time will vary depending on the amount of natural pectin and sugar in the fruit.

Remove from the heat and pour the jam into the sterilized jars, cover, and vacuum-seal as directed on page 86. Let stand for 24 hours before serving or giving.

Strawberry–
Grand Marnier Jam

UTENSILS NEEDED: Heavy-bottomed nonstick saucepan;
for preserving, four 8-ounce canning jars with lids, sterilized;
for refrigerating, four 8-ounce containers with lids, sterilized

COOKING TIME: Approximately 30 minutes

QUANTITY: Four 8-ounce containers

STORAGE: Vacuum-sealed jars last 1 year;
refrigerated, up to 4 weeks.

INGREDIENTS

*4½ cups fresh
strawberries,
preferably organic,
washed, dried,
and hulled*

3 cups sugar

*¼ cup Grand Marnier
liqueur*

Combine the strawberries and sugar in a heavy-bottomed nonstick saucepan over medium-high heat and, while stirring constantly, bring to a boil. Continue to cook, stirring constantly, for 30 minutes, or until the mixture thickens to the consistency of jam.

Remove from the heat and stir in the Grand Marnier. Immediately pour the jam into the sterilized containers, cover, and vacuum-seal as directed on page 86, or pour into containers, cover, and set aside to cool before refrigerating.

Papaya-Lime Jam

2 cups sugar

2 cups water

¼ cup freshly squeezed
   lime juice

1 tablespoon freshly
   grated lime zest

¼ teaspoon ground
   cinnamon

3 cups fresh, barely
   ripe papaya chunks
   (see Note)

UTENSILS NEEDED: Heavy-bottomed nonstick saucepan; for preserving,
four 8-ounce canning jars and lids, sterilized; for refrigerating,
four 8-ounce containers with lids, sterilized

COOKING TIME: Approximately 45 minutes

QUANTITY: Four 8-ounce containers

STORAGE: Vacuum-sealed jars last 1 year; refrigerated, up to 1 month.

––––––––––––––

Combine the sugar, water, lime juice, lime zest, and cinnamon in a heavy-bottomed nonstick saucepan over high heat. Stirring constantly, bring to a boil. Continue to boil for 5 minutes.

Add the papaya, lower the heat, and gently simmer for 40 minutes, or until the papaya is translucent.

Remove from the heat, and immediately pour the jam into the sterilized jars, cover, and vacuum-seal as directed on page 86, or pour into containers, cover, and set aside to cool before refrigerating.

NOTE: Papaya may be replaced with pawpaw (aka papaw) if it is native to your locale.

Papaya Lime Jam

Tomato-Basil Jam

UTENSILS NEEDED: Small bowl; heavy-bottomed nonstick saucepan; metal spoon; for preserving, four 8-ounce canning jars with lids, sterilized; for refrigerating, four 8-ounce containers with lids, sterilized

BOILING TIME: 1 minute

QUANTITY: Four 8-ounce containers

STORAGE: Vacuum-sealed jars last 1 year; refrigerated, up to 1 month.

INGREDIENTS

3 cups sugar

1 1.75-ounce packet light powdered pectin

4 cups peeled, seeded, and chopped fresh tomatoes

¾ cup chopped fresh basil leaves and stems

¼ cup freshly squeezed lemon juice

Combine ¾ cup of the sugar with the pectin in a small bowl. Set aside.

Combine the tomatoes, basil, and lemon juice in a heavy-bottomed nonstick saucepan over medium-high heat. Stir in the sugar-pectin mixture and, while stirring constantly, bring to a full, rolling boil. Add the remaining 2¼ cups sugar and, stirring constantly, again bring the mixture to a full, rolling boil. Continue to boil, stirring constantly, for 1 minute.

Remove from the heat and, using a metal spoon, skim off and discard any foam that rises to the top. Immediately pour the jam into the sterilized jars, cover, and vacuum-seal as directed on page 86, or pour into containers, cover, and set aside to cool before refrigerating.

Microwave Marmalade

UTENSILS NEEDED: Food processor fitted with the metal blade; microwavable bowl; 1-cup storage container with lid, sterilized

MICROWAVE TIME: Approximately 6 minutes

SETTING TIME: 8 hours

QUANTITY: Approximately 1 cup

STORAGE: Keep in an airtight container, refrigerated, up to 10 days.

INGREDIENTS

1 large orange, 1 medium grapefruit, 2 large lemons, or 2 large limes, preferably organic, washed, blemishes cut off, and seeds removed

Sugar to equal fruit (see below)

Cut the citrus (with peel) into pieces and place in the bowl of a food processor fitted with the metal blade. Pulse until coarsely chopped.

Scrape the fruit from the bowl and measure it exactly. Place it in a microwavable bowl.

Measure a volume of sugar equal to that of the fruit. Add the sugar to the fruit and stir to mix well.

Place the bowl in the center of a microwave oven and cook on medium, stirring twice, for about 6 minutes, until the liquid becomes thick and syrupy. Do not overcook, or the fruit will be soggy.

Remove from the microwave and place the marmalade in a clean container with a lid. Cover and refrigerate for 8 hours before serving.

Blood Orange Marmalade

INGREDIENTS

8 blood oranges, washed,
  seeded, and chopped

2 lemons, washed, seeded,
  and chopped

Water to equal fruit
  (see below)

Sugar to equal fruit
  (see below)

UTENSILS NEEDED: Measuring cup; heavy-bottomed nonstick saucepan;
for preserving, twelve 4-ounce canning jars with lids, sterilized; for refrigerating,
twelve 4-ounce containers with lids, sterilized

COOKING TIME: Approximately 55 minutes total

RESTING TIME: 2 days

QUANTITY: Twelve 4-ounce containers

STORAGE: Vacuum-sealed jars last 1 year; refrigerated, up to 6 weeks.

Measure the chopped fruit in a measuring cup and place in a heavy-bottomed nonstick saucepan. Measure an equal volume of cold water and add it to the fruit. Place over medium-high heat and bring to a boil. Lower the heat and simmer for 5 minutes.

Remove from the heat. Cover and set aside for 24 hours.

Uncover and again place the saucepan over medium-high heat. Bring to a boil and boil for 10 minutes.

Remove from the heat. Cover and set aside for another 24 hours.

Measure the fruit mixture in a measuring cup and return the measured amount to the saucepan. Measure an equal volume of sugar and add it to the saucepan. Place over medium-high heat and bring to a boil. Lower the heat and simmer, stirring frequently, for about 40 minutes, or until the fruit is tender and the syrup thickens.

Remove from the heat and allow to rest for 10 minutes. Ladle into the sterilized jars, cover, and vacuum-seal as directed on page 86, or ladle into the containers, cover, and set aside to cool before refrigerating.

Pumpkin-Ginger Marmalade

UTENSILS NEEDED: Juicer; measuring cup; nonreactive bowl; small saucepan; heavy-bottomed nonstick saucepan; slotted spoon; for preserving, six 8-ounce canning jars and lids, sterilized; for refrigerating, six 8-ounce containers with lids, sterilized

COOKING TIME: Approximately 70 minutes

RESTING TIME: 12 hours

QUANTITY: Six 8-ounce containers

STORAGE: Vacuum-sealed jars last 1 year; refrigerated, up to 1 month.

INGREDIENTS

6 lemons, washed

1 small pumpkin (about 4 pounds), peeled, seeded, and sliced into thin ½-inch squares

Sugar to equal pumpkin (see below)

¼ cup freshly grated ginger

Juice the lemons, discarding the seeds and reserving the juice and the rinds separately.

Measure the pumpkin pieces in a measuring cup and then measure an equal volume of sugar. Combine the pumpkin pieces and sugar with the ginger and reserved lemon juice in a nonreactive bowl. Cover and let stand for 12 hours.

When the pumpkin is ready, chop the lemon rinds and place them in a small saucepan over high heat. Add cold water to cover by 1 inch. Place over medium heat and bring to a boil. Lower heat and simmer for about 15 minutes, or until the rinds are tender.

Remove from the heat, drain well, and set aside.

Place the pumpkin mixture in a large, heavy-bottomed nonstick saucepan over high heat. Lower the heat and simmer for about 35 minutes, or until the pumpkin is translucent.

Remove from the heat and, using a slotted spoon, lift the pumpkin pieces from the syrup and set aside.

Return the pumpkin syrup to high heat and bring to a full, rolling boil. Continue to boil for about 15 minutes, or until the syrup thickens slightly. Return the pumpkin to the boiling syrup, along with the reserved lemon rind. Return the mixture to a boil and continue to boil for 5 minutes.

Remove from the heat and immediately pour the marmalade into sterilized jars, cover, and vacuum-seal as directed on page 86, or pour into sterilized containers, cover, and set aside to cool before refrigerating.

6

SYRUPS & SWEET SAUCES

SYRUPS MAY BE USED AS TOPPINGS FOR BREAKFAST TREATS such as waffles and pancakes, with ice cream, as cake glazes, and in drinks. They are generally made from fruit purée or juice, spices, or liqueurs.

Sweet sauces are, for the most part, used as toppings for ice cream, cakes, puddings, or fruit. Occasionally, a sweet sauce is used as an accompaniment to or as a basting sauce for meats, poultry, or game. These sauces may be made from chopped or puréed fruit or vegetables, chocolate, citrus, or liqueur bases.

Syrups and dessert sauces can be preserved by the open-kettle method and vacuum-sealed with rubber-edged rings and screw caps, as directed on page 86. All may be refrigerated for short-term storage or, occasionally, frozen. Some must be reheated before serving.

For gift giving, I often pack syrups in old wine or soda bottles, label them, and tie a raffia or ribbon bow around the neck of the bottle. Dessert sauces can be packed in reusable lidded glass containers and accompanied by a new or antique spoon or scoop. For a little something extra, syrups can be made into gift packages with a pancake or waffle mix or, when unusual, with an item appropriate to its use.

SYRUPS

Spiced Blueberry Syrup

Framboise Syrup

Fresh Herb Syrup

SWEET SAUCES

Praline Sauce

Killer Chocolate Fudge Sauce

Bittersweet Chocolate Sauce

Sambuca Sauce

Spiced Blueberry Syrup

INGREDIENTS

*4 cups fresh blueberries,
picked clean, washed,
and dried*

*1 cup sugar, plus more to
taste*

*½ cup freshly squeezed
lemon juice*

*½ cup freshly squeezed
orange juice*

*1 teaspoon ground
cinnamon*

*½ teaspoon Chinese five-
spice powder*

*¼ teaspoon freshly grated
nutmeg*

*2 tablespoons cornstarch
dissolved in ¼ cup
cold water*

*½ cup (1 stick) unsalted
butter, cut into pieces,
at room temperature*

UTENSILS NEEDED: Heavy-bottomed nonstick saucepan; whisk; for preserving, four 8-ounce canning jars or bottles with lids, sterilized; for refrigerating, four 8-ounce containers with lids, sterilized

COOKING TIME: Approximately 25 minutes

QUANTITY: Four 8-ounce containers

STORAGE: Vacuum-sealed jars last 1 year; refrigerated, up to 6 weeks. May be frozen.

SERVING SUGGESTIONS: Breakfast or dessert topping; glaze for pork or game

---

Combine the blueberries with the sugar, lemon and orange juices, cinnamon, five-spice powder, and nutmeg in a heavy-bottomed nonstick saucepan over medium-high heat. Stirring constantly, bring to a boil. Lower the heat and simmer, stirring occasionally, for 20 minutes. Taste for sweetness and, if necessary, add more sugar to taste. If adding sugar, cook for an additional 5 minutes.

Whisk in the cornstarch mixture and continue to cook, stirring constantly, for about 5 minutes, or until thickened. Whisk in the butter, a bit at a time.

Remove from the heat and immediately pour the syrup into sterilized jars, cover, and vacuum-seal as directed on page 86, or pour into sterilized containers, cover, and refrigerate.

NOTE: If you object to blueberry seeds in your syrup, strain the mixture through a fine-mesh sieve after the initial 20 minutes of cooking. Return the strained syrup to a saucepan and bring to a boil before whisking in the cornstarch mixture.

Framboise Syrup

UTENSILS NEEDED: Heavy-bottomed saucepan; saucepan; fine-mesh sieve lined with cheesecloth; metal spoon; for preserving, two 12-ounce canning jars or bottles with lids, sterilized; for refrigerating, two 12-ounce containers with lids, sterilized

COOKING TIME: Approximately 15 minutes

QUANTITY: Two 12-ounce containers

STORAGE: Vacuum-sealed jars last 1 year; refrigerated, up to 6 weeks.

INGREDIENTS

Three 10-ounce packages frozen raspberries, thawed

½ cup framboise or other raspberry brandy

2 cups sugar

½ cup freshly squeezed orange juice

Combine the raspberries with the framboise in a heavy-bottomed saucepan over medium heat. Stir in the sugar and orange juice and bring to a boil. Lower the heat and simmer for 15 minutes.

Remove from the heat and strain into a clean saucepan through a fine-mesh sieve lined with cheesecloth. Place over medium heat and bring to a boil. Using a metal spoon, skim off any foam that rises to the top.

Remove from the heat and immediately pour the syrup into sterilized jars or bottles, cover, and vacuum-seal as directed on page 86, or pour into sterilized containers, cover, and refrigerate.

Fresh Herb Syrup

UTENSILS NEEDED: Two saucepans; fine-mesh sieve lined with cheesecloth;
four 8-ounce containers with lids, sterilized

COOKING TIME: Approximately 10 minutes

RESTING TIME: 12 hours

QUANTITY: Four 8-ounce containers

STORAGE: Refrigerated jars last up to 1 month.

SERVING SUGGESTIONS: Sweetener for iced tea; glaze for plain cake or pound cake

INGREDIENTS

2 cups dry white wine

2 cups water

2 cups sugar

2 cups chopped fresh
herbs (rosemary, sage,
and/or thyme)

Combine the wine, water, and sugar in a saucepan
set over medium heat. Add the herbs and bring to
a boil. Lower the heat and simmer for 10 minutes.

Remove from the heat and set aside for
about 1 hour or until cool. Cover and let stand
for 12 hours.

Strain into a clean saucepan through a
fine-mesh sieve lined with cheesecloth. Place
over medium heat and bring to a simmer.

Remove from the heat and pour into
sterilized containers, cover, and refrigerate.

Praline Sauce

UTENSILS NEEDED: Heavy-bottomed nonstick saucepan;
four 8-ounce containers with lids, sterilized

COOKING TIME: Approximately 22 minutes

QUANTITY: Four 8-ounce containers

STORAGE: Cover tightly and refrigerate up to 1 month.

Combine the egg yolks, brown sugar, and butter in a heavy-bottomed nonstick saucepan over low heat. Cook, stirring constantly, for about 7 minutes, or until well blended. Beat in the cream and bourbon and cook, stirring constantly, for about 10 minutes, or until thick. Stir in the pecans and cook for an additional 5 minutes.

Remove from the heat and immediately pour the sauce into sterilized containers, cover, and refrigerate. Reheat before serving.

INGREDIENTS

8 large egg yolks, at room temperature, beaten

1 cup light brown sugar

¼ cup (½ stick) unsalted butter, at room temperature

1 cup heavy cream

¼ cup bourbon or other fine whiskey

3 cups toasted pecans

Killer Chocolate Fudge Sauce

UTENSILS NEEDED: Double boiler; four 8-ounce containers with lids, sterilized

COOKING TIME: Approximately 10 minutes

QUANTITY: Four 8-ounce containers

STORAGE: Cover tightly and refrigerate up to 1 month or freeze up to 6 months.

Place the chocolate in the top half of a double boiler over boiling water. Heat, stirring constantly, until melted. Stir in the beaten egg yolks, brown sugar, and orange zest. Cook, stirring constantly, for about 5 minutes, or until well blended. Beat in the butter, heavy cream, and, if using, liqueur. Continue to cook, stirring constantly, for an additional 5 minutes.

Remove from the heat and pour the sauce into sterilized containers, cover, and refrigerate or freeze. Reheat before using.

INGREDIENTS

4 ounces fine-quality unsweetened chocolate, cut into pieces

6 large egg yolks, at room temperature, beaten

½ cup light brown sugar

1 tablespoon freshly grated orange zest

½ cup (1 stick) unsalted butter, at room temperature

¼ cup heavy cream

¼ cup liqueur of choice, optional

Bittersweet Chocolate Sauce

INGREDIENTS

12 ounces fine-quality
  bittersweet chocolate,
  cut into pieces

¾ cup espresso or any
  other intensely
  flavored coffee

2 cups (4 sticks) unsalted
  butter, cut into pieces
  and chilled

2 teaspoons pure vanilla
  extract

UTENSILS NEEDED: Heavy-bottomed nonstick saucepan;
four 4-ounce containers with lids, sterilized

COOKING TIME: Approximately 5 minutes

QUANTITY: Four 4-ounce containers

STORAGE: Cover tightly and refrigerate up to 2 weeks.

SERVING SUGGESTIONS: Use warm as a dessert sauce; use cold
as a frosting for cakes or cupcakes.

Combine the chocolate with the espresso in a heavy-bottomed nonstick saucepan over medium heat. Cook, stirring constantly, for about 5 minutes, or until the chocolate is melted and the mixture is blended. If the chocolate begins to stick, remove the pan from the heat, lower the heat, and then return the pan to the heat and continue stirring to blend.

Remove the chocolate mixture from the heat and beat in the butter, a few pieces at a time, beating until all of the butter is added and the sauce is rich and thick. If the sauce gets too cool before all of the butter is added, return it to low heat and cook, stirring constantly, for a couple of minutes, or until the sauce is hot. Do not add butter while the sauce is on the heat, or the sauce will begin to separate.

When all of the butter is added, beat in the vanilla and immediately pour the sauce into sterilized containers, cover, and refrigerate.

Sambuca Sauce

UTENSILS NEEDED: Double boiler; wooden spoon;
three 8-ounce containers with lids, sterilized

COOKING TIME: Approximately 16 minutes

QUANTITY: Three 8-ounce containers

STORAGE: Cover tightly and refrigerate up to 1 month or freeze up to 6 months.

Combine the bittersweet chocolate and butter in the top half of a double boiler over simmering water. Heat, stirring constantly with a wooden spoon, for about 5 minutes, or until blended. Beat in the cocoa and espresso powders and then, stirring constantly, beat in the brown sugar and half-and-half. Cook, stirring constantly, for about 10 minutes, or until the sauce is thick. Beat in the Sambuca and chocolate nibs and cook for 1 additional minute.

Remove from the heat and immediately pour the sauce into sterilized containers, cover, and refrigerate. Reheat before serving.

NOTE: Chocolate nibs, which are bits of processed cocoa beans, are available from bakery supply companies and at some specialty food stores.

INGREDIENTS

4 ounces fine-quality bittersweet chocolate, cut into pieces

⅔ cup unsalted butter

¼ cup Dutch-process cocoa powder

¼ cup instant espresso powder

1 cup light brown sugar

⅓ cup half-and-half

⅓ cup Sambuca Romana liqueur

½ cup chocolate nibs (see Note)

7

SPICED FRUITS & CHUTNEYS

SPICED FRUITS ARE WHOLE FRUITS or, less frequently, uniform slices or pieces of fruit—either one type or mixed—cooked in a (usually) sweet, spicy syrup until plump and aromatic. The fruit retains its shape but takes on some of the color of the spice. Also known as pickled fruits, they are a unique and flavorful accompaniment to meat, poultry, or game. Spiced fruits may also be successfully used as dessert.

Before processing, sterilized jars are filled with the food to be preserved, leaving ½-inch headspace in each filled jar (unless otherwise specified). Air bubbles are removed by pushing around the inside edge of the jar with a rubber spatula. The sealing edges are wiped clean with a dry cloth or paper towel before covering with a lid and screw cap. The lids are not tightly sealed to allow for expansion.

Many spiced fruits require a 10-minute boiling water bath for completion of the preserving process. The jars are always placed on a wire rack set on the bottom of the pot, allowing free circulation of the boiling water around and under each jar. The water should be brought to a boil as quickly as possible and then the heat should be lowered to keep the water at a steady, quiet boil. The processing time begins at the moment the water is at the boil.

When processing is complete, the jars are lifted from the water bath with tongs. The jars are then wiped dry, the screw caps tightened, and the jars inverted for 10 minutes to test for leaks. Then the jars are transferred (now upright) to wire racks to cool before storing in a cool, dry spot.

Chutneys are hot, spicy-sweet mixed chopped fruit or vegetable jam-pickles. They can be exceedingly spicy, but the degree of heat may be adjusted to individual taste. Authentically served with Indian curries, chutneys are also compatible with non-Indian meats, poultry, and fish dishes.

Chutneys are usually made by the open-kettle method and vacuum-sealed as described on page 86.

Both spiced fruits and chutneys may be placed in sterilized containers, covered, and refrigerated for a short period of time or frozen for up to 12 months.

Because many spiced fruits and chutneys are unusual, when giving them as gifts it is always a good idea to accompany them with ideas for use. They also lend themselves to unusual containers instead of the familiar canning jars. Crocks, carafes, lovely old glass jars or dishes with lids, and containers that express the country the recipe comes from are just a few of the receptacles I might use when preparing these treats to give.

Spiced Cherries

UTENSILS NEEDED: Deep glass bowl or crock with lid; fine-mesh sieve; measuring cup; four 8-ounce canning jars with lids, sterilized

MARINATION TIME: Nearly 5 weeks

QUANTITY: Four 8-ounce jars

STORAGE: Keep in a cool, dark spot or refrigerator up to 6 months.

SERVING SUGGESTIONS: Use as a garnish for meat, poultry, or game; as an hors d'oeuvre; and in place of olives in drinks or on relish trays.

INGREDIENTS

6 cups ripe, firm Bing, Queen Anne, or sour cherries, some preferably with stems, washed and dried

Champagne wine vinegar

Sugar to equal fruit (see below)

2-inch piece fresh ginger, peeled and sliced

¼ cup ground cinnamon

½ teaspoon ground cloves

Four 2-inch pieces cinnamon stick

Place the cherries in a deep glass bowl or crock with a lid. Pour in enough vinegar to cover the cherries by 1 inch, cover, and place in a cool, dark spot for 3 days.

Uncover the cherries and drain through a fine-mesh sieve, separately reserving both the liquid and the cherries.

Measure the cherries in a measuring cup and return them to the glass bowl or crock. Measure an equal volume of sugar and add it to the bowl. Add the ginger, ground cinnamon, and cloves, stirring to coat the cherries. Again, cover and place in a cool, dark spot for another 3 days, giving the cherries a good stir once each day.

Pour the marinated cherries into hot, sterilized jars and add a piece of cinnamon stick to each jar. Cover tightly and place in a cool, dark spot or in the refrigerator for 4 weeks before serving.

Peaches in Port Wine

INGREDIENTS

3 cups water

3 cups port wine

2½ cups sugar

*2½ tablespoons freshly
    squeezed lemon juice*

*One 3 × ½-inch strip
    lemon peel*

*One 3 × ½-inch strip
    orange peel*

*20 medium ripe peaches,
    peeled*

12 whole cloves

*Four 4-inch pieces
    cinnamon stick*

*1 tablespoon white
    peppercorns*

UTENSILS NEEDED: Large heavy-bottomed nonstick pot;
four 16-ounce canning jars with lids, sterilized

COOKING TIME: 10 minutes plus 10-minute boiling water bath

QUANTITY: Four 16-ounce jars

STORAGE: Vacuum-sealed jars last 1 year; refrigerated, up to 1 month.

SERVING SUGGESTIONS: Use as a condiment or as a garnish for roasted meat or poultry.
Serve as a light dessert with butter cookies.

Combine the water and port wine in a large heavy-bottomed nonstick pot. Place over medium-high heat and stir in the sugar. When the sugar is dissolved, stir in the lemon juice and the lemon and orange peels. Add the peaches, cloves, cinnamon sticks, and peppercorns and bring to a boil, stirring occasionally. Lower the heat and simmer for 10 minutes.

Remove from the heat and pack the peaches into the sterilized jars, dividing evenly. Pour the syrup and spices over the peaches in each jar, leaving ¼-inch headspace, and making sure each jar has a piece of cinnamon stick and some cloves and peppercorns. Cover and place in a boiling water bath. Process for 10 minutes, remove from the water bath, and cool according to the directions on page 109.

Preserved Lemons

UTENSILS NEEDED: Glass bowl; four 8-ounce glass or ceramic containers with glass or plastic lids, sterilized (see Note)

MARINATION TIME: 1 week

QUANTITY: Four 8-ounce containers

STORAGE: Cover tightly and refrigerate up to 6 months.

SERVING SUGGESTIONS: Essential ingredient in many Moroccan dishes; use as a garnish and/or seasoning for salads and grain dishes.

INGREDIENTS

12 Meyer or organic lemons, washed and dried

1⅓ cups coarse salt

2 cups freshly squeezed lemon juice

Approximately 1 cup extra-virgin olive oil

Cut each lemon lengthwise into 8 equal wedges and place them in a glass bowl. Add the salt and toss to coat.

Firmly pack the salted lemon pieces into the sterilized containers. Add an equal portion of lemon juice to each container, cover, and set aside in a cool, dark spot to marinate for 1 week. Shake each jar once a day.

At the end of the week, open the containers and add enough extra-virgin olive oil to fill the container with liquid. Cover and refrigerate for up to 6 months.

NOTE: You don't want to use metal lids since the acid will interact with the metal and cause an off taste as well as change the color of the lemons.

Cranberry Chutney

INGREDIENTS

1 large green apple, peeled, cored, and chopped

6 cups chopped fresh or frozen cranberries

1 cup chopped red onion

1 cup dried currants

½ cup chopped celery

1½ tablespoons minced garlic

1 tablespoon minced fresh ginger

2½ cups light brown sugar

¾ cup dry red wine

1 teaspoon ground cinnamon

½ teaspoon ground cloves

½ teaspoon ground cardamom

¼ teaspoon cayenne pepper

UTENSILS NEEDED: Heavy-bottomed nonstick saucepan; for preserving, six 8-ounce canning jars with lids, sterilized; for refrigerating, six 8-ounce containers with lids, sterilized

COOKING TIME: 30 minutes

QUANTITY: Six 8-ounce containers

STORAGE: Vacuum-sealed jars last 1 year; refrigerated, up to 6 weeks. May be frozen.

SERVING SUGGESTION: As a condiment for roast meats, poultry, or sandwiches.

Combine the apple, cranberries, onion, currants, celery, garlic, and ginger in a heavy-bottomed nonstick saucepan. Stir in the brown sugar. Add the wine, cinnamon, cloves, cardamom, and cayenne and bring to a boil over medium-high heat. Lower the heat and simmer, stirring frequently, for 30 minutes, or until the mixture is thick and the flavors are blended.

Remove from the heat and pack into the sterilized jars, cover, and vacuum-seal as directed on page 86 before cooling and storing.

Mango-Lime Chutney

UTENSILS NEEDED: Heavy-bottomed nonstick saucepan; for preserving,
four 8-ounce canning jars and lids, sterilized; for refrigerating,
four 8-ounce containers with lids, sterilized

COOKING TIME: 35 minutes total

RESTING TIME: 12 hours

QUANTITY: Four 8-ounce containers

STORAGE: Vacuum-sealed jars last 1 year; refrigerated, up to 6 weeks. May be frozen.

SERVING SUGGESTIONS: As a garnish for curries, roast poultry, pork, or lamb,
or as a sandwich condiment.

INGREDIENTS

4 cups peeled, pitted, and sliced firm, ripe mango

1 cup chopped yellow onion

¾ cup golden seedless raisins

½ cup seeded and chopped lime (rind included)

½ cup chopped fresh ginger

¼ cup minced garlic

1 tablespoon minced fresh red or green chile pepper, or to taste

1 tablespoon mustard seeds

1 teaspoon ground cinnamon

½ teaspoon ground cloves

2 cups light brown sugar

1 cup white wine vinegar

¼ cup freshly squeezed orange juice

¼ cup freshly squeezed lemon juice

Combine the mango, onion, raisins, lime, ginger, garlic, chile pepper, mustard seeds, cinnamon, and cloves in a heavy-bottomed nonstick saucepan over medium heat. Add the brown sugar, vinegar, and orange and lemon juices. Stirring frequently, bring to a boil. Lower the heat and simmer for 20 minutes.

Remove from the heat, cover, and set aside to rest for 12 hours.

Keep covered and return to medium-high heat. Bring to a boil, then lower the heat and simmer for 15 minutes.

Remove from the heat and pack in the sterilized jars, cover, and vacuum-seal as directed on page 86, or pack into containers, cover, and set aside to cool before refrigerating or freezing.

8

RELISHES, PICKLES & OLIVES

RELISHES ARE MADE OF FINELY SLICED, shredded, or chopped vegetables or fruits, or a combination of vegetables and fruits. They may be either sweet or savory, spicy or mild, and are usually seasoned with vinegars, spices, and herbs. Considered old-fashioned, relishes have only recently been rediscovered as a wonderful accompaniment to meat, poultry, and game, or as a dressing on sandwiches.

Pickles are also made from both vegetables and fruits, which may be left whole, sliced, chopped, or sectioned (and peeled, if necessary), depending on the type of pickle desired. Vegetables are generally pickled with salt or vinegar, or with a combination of salt, vinegar, and spices. Fruits are usually pickled with vinegar, other acids, sugar, and spices. Unless otherwise directed, whole spices used for seasoning should be tied in a cheesecloth bag and removed before the pickles are bottled. Some pickles are crunchy and crisp, while others are still firm but have lost their crispness through cooking.

For all crisp pickles, I use coarse (or kosher) salt or large-grained sea salt and white distilled or champagne wine vinegar. Slightly underripe vegetables or fruits remain crunchier when pickled.

Relishes are usually preserved using the open-kettle method. Pickles are often preserved without cooking, but the open-kettle and boiling water bath methods can also be used. Both relishes and pickles can be placed in airtight containers, covered, and refrigerated for about a month, but most do not freeze well.

Olives, unless you are lucky enough to find fresh ones, have already been cured, so they require very little preparation. They store beautifully for a month or two in the refrigerator. Olive recipes are great for inexperienced cooks because with just a little effort and almost no skill you can create a very tasty gift from the kitchen.

These homemade items lend themselves to being packed in lots of different containers—crocks, covered glass jars or bowls, and condiment dishes are just a few ideas. Pickles and relishes can be packed together in baskets, on trays, or in a fancy box for a marvelous and most welcome gift.

Thai Cucumber Relish

NO COOKING

UTENSILS NEEDED: Glass mixing bowl; four 8-ounce containers and lids, sterilized

QUANTITY: Four 8-ounce jars

STORAGE: Refrigerate in an airtight container up to 2 weeks.

SERVING SUGGESTIONS: Use as a salad or garnish for Thai or other Asian-inspired entrées, or as a picnic salad.

Combine the cucumbers, mint, garlic, lemongrass, and chile in a glass bowl. Stir in the vinegar and sake. Add the sugar and stir to dissolve. Season with salt to taste.

Place in sterilized containers, cover, and refrigerate until ready to serve or give.

INGREDIENTS

10 hothouse cucumbers, washed and chopped

1 large bunch fresh mint leaves, washed and chopped

2 tablespoons minced garlic

2 tablespoons minced lemongrass

1 tablespoon minced hot red chile pepper

2 cups rice wine vinegar

½ cup sake

¼ cup superfine sugar

Coarse salt to taste

Sun-Dried Tomato Relish

INGREDIENTS

8 cups tomato purée

1 dried red hot chile pepper

1 bay leaf

One 3-inch piece cinnamon stick

2 teaspoons mustard seeds

2 teaspoons black peppercorns

1 teaspoon ground allspice

¾ cup light brown sugar

2 tablespoons balsamic vinegar

1½ teaspoons coarse salt, or to taste

½ teaspoon hot paprika

2 cups sliced oil-packed sun-dried tomatoes, well drained

½ cup chopped fresh basil leaves

½ cup red wine vinegar

UTENSILS NEEDED: Heavy-bottomed nonstick saucepan; cheesecloth bag; for preserving, six 8-ounce canning jars and lids, sterilized; for refrigerating, six 8-ounce containers and lids, sterilized

COOKING TIME: About 1 hour total

QUANTITY: Six 8-ounce containers

STORAGE: Vacuum-sealed jars last 1 year; refrigerated, up to 3 months. May be frozen.

SERVING SUGGESTIONS: Use as a garnish or condiment for grilled or roasted meat, game, or poultry, or as a sandwich dressing.

Place the tomato purée in a heavy-bottomed nonstick saucepan over medium heat and bring to a simmer. Continue to simmer, stirring occasionally, for about 30 minutes, or until reduced by one-half.

Tie the dried chile, bay leaf, cinnamon stick, mustard seeds, peppercorns, and allspice in a cheesecloth bag. Add the bag to the reduced purée. Stir in the brown sugar, balsamic vinegar, salt, and paprika and bring to a boil. Lower the heat and simmer for an additional 20 minutes, or until reduced by one-third.

Raise the heat and stir in the sun-dried tomatoes, basil, and red wine vinegar and again bring to a boil. Lower the heat and simmer, stirring frequently, for 10 minutes. Taste and, if necessary, add salt.

Remove from the heat and discard the spice bag. Immediately pour the relish into the sterilized jars, cover, and vacuum-seal as directed on page 86, or pour into sterilized containers, cover, and set aside to cool before refrigerating or freezing.

Fresh Fig Relish

UTENSILS NEEDED: Mixing bowl; heavy-bottomed nonstick saucepan;
cheesecloth bag; four 4-ounce canning jars and lids, sterilized

MARINATING TIME: 3 hours

COOKING TIME: 30 minutes

QUANTITY: Four 4-ounce jars

STORAGE: Vacuum-sealed jars last 1 year.

SERVING SUGGESTION: Use as a garnish for meat, poultry, game, or curries.

INGREDIENTS

3 pounds fresh ripe figs, washed, stemmed, and cut crosswise into thin slices

2 cups sugar

½ cup freshly squeezed orange juice

1 teaspoon freshly grated orange zest

½ teaspoon freshly grated lemon zest

6 whole cloves

2 whole allspice berries

1 cinnamon stick, chopped into pieces

½ cup sherry wine vinegar

1 cup toasted slivered almonds

¼ cup dried currants

Combine the figs with the sugar in a mixing bowl, tossing to coat. Add the orange juice and the orange and lemon zest. Cover and set aside to marinate for 3 hours.

Transfer the marinated figs and all of the juice to a heavy-bottomed nonstick saucepan. Set over medium heat. Tie the cloves, allspice, and cinnamon stick pieces in a cheesecloth bag and add it to the saucepan. Bring to a boil, then lower the heat and add the vinegar. Simmer for about 30 minutes, or until very thick.

Remove from the heat and stir in the almonds and currants. Immediately pour the relish into sterilized jars, cover, and vacuum-seal as directed on page 86.

Tuscan Onions

INGREDIENTS

5 pounds blanched red
or white pearl onions,
skins removed, or
large red onions,
peeled and sliced

¼ cup olive oil

¼ cup balsamic vinegar

¼ cup dry red wine

2 tablespoons light brown
sugar

2 teaspoons chopped fresh
rosemary

1 teaspoon chopped fresh
thyme

Coarse salt and freshly
ground pepper, to taste

1 cup golden seedless
raisins

1 cup toasted pine nuts

PREHEAT OVEN TO: 350°F

UTENSILS NEEDED: Baking sheet; aluminum foil; small sharp knife;
heatproof bowl; six 8-ounce containers with lids, sterilized

BAKING TIME: Approximately 45 minutes

QUANTITY: Six 8-ounce containers

STORAGE: Refrigerate in an airtight container up to 2 weeks.

SERVING SUGGESTIONS: Use warm, chilled, or at room temperature as a garnish for
meat, poultry, or game, or use as a condiment for meat sandwiches.

———————

Combine the onions with the olive oil, vinegar, red wine, brown sugar, rosemary, thyme, salt, and pepper on a baking sheet, tossing to coat well. Cover tightly with aluminum foil and bake for about 45 minutes, or until the onions are very tender when pierced with the point of a small sharp knife.

While the onions are roasting, place the raisins in a small heatproof bowl and cover with boiling water. Soak for about 10 minutes, or until the raisins are plumped slightly. Drain well and set aside.

When the onions are tender, remove them from the oven and add the pine nuts and the reserved raisins. Toss to combine. Transfer to sterilized containers, cover, and set aside to cool before refrigerating.

Cured Wild Mushrooms

*2½ pounds mixed wild
mushrooms, or a
combination of wild
and domestic
mushrooms, trimmed
of stems and bruised
parts, rinsed clean
(see Note)*

*2 cups extra-virgin olive
oil*

1 cup tarragon vinegar

*3 tablespoons freshly
grated onion*

*1 tablespoon roasted
garlic purée (see
page 20)*

½ teaspoon sugar

8 cloves garlic, peeled

*8 sprigs fresh basil,
washed and dried*

*1 teaspoon crushed red
pepper flakes*

NO COOKING

UTENSILS NEEDED: Large glass mixing bowl;
four 16-ounce containers with lids, sterilized

MARINATING TIME: 24 hours

QUANTITY: Four 16-ounce containers

STORAGE: Refrigerate in an airtight container up to 3 months.

SERVING SUGGESTIONS: Use as an appetizer or an hors d'oeuvre, a salad ingredient,
or a garnish for meat, poultry, or game.

———————

Combine the mushrooms with the olive oil, vinegar, onion, garlic purée, and sugar in a glass mixing bowl, stirring to combine. Set aside for 10 minutes, or until the sugar is dissolved.

Place 2 garlic cloves, 2 basil sprigs, and an equal portion of the red pepper flakes in each sterilized container. Pack each jar with mushrooms and add liquid to cover. Cover and refrigerate for at least 24 hours before serving or giving.

NOTE: If using wild mushrooms, a quick rinse will ensure that any forest debris or insects are washed away. Domestic mushrooms can be brushed clean.

Easy Pickles

NO COOKING

UTENSILS NEEDED: Large nonreactive bowl;
four 1-quart canning jars with lids or other glass
containers with lids, sterilized

RESTING TIME: 3 days

QUANTITY: Four 1-quart jars

STORAGE: Refrigerate in an airtight container
up to 3 months.

Combine the cucumbers, chiles, and garlic cloves in a large nonreactive bowl. Add the sugar and salt, tossing to combine. Add the vinegar and water and set aside, stirring occasionally, for about 30 minutes, or until the sugar and salt are dissolved.

Pack the cucumbers into the sterilized jars, adding an equal number of garlic cloves, 1 chile, and 3 dill sprigs to each jar. Pour in enough liquid to cover the cucumbers. Cover and refrigerate for at least 3 days before serving or giving.

NOTE: If the cucumbers are very large, cut them into quarters lengthwise.

INGREDIENTS

*4½ pounds kirby
(pickling) cucumbers,
washed (see Note)*

*4 dried hot red chile
peppers*

*1 head garlic, pulled into
cloves and peeled*

1 cup sugar

*3 tablespoons coarse salt,
or to taste*

*4 cups distilled white
vinegar*

4 cups water

12 sprigs fresh dill

Mediterranean Olives

NO COOKING

UTENSILS NEEDED: Mixing bowl;
four 8-ounce containers with lids, sterilized

MARINATING TIME: 1 week

QUANTITY: Four 8-ounce containers

STORAGE: Refrigerate in an airtight container
up to 3 months.

INGREDIENTS

4 cups mixed Italian or Greek black and green olives

2 tablespoons dried red pepper flakes

2 tablespoons minced garlic

1 tablespoon freshly grated orange zest

2 teaspoons minced fresh rosemary

1 teaspoon fines herbes

¼ cup balsamic vinegar

Approximately 2 cups extra-virgin olive oil

Combine the olives with the red pepper flakes, garlic, orange zest, rosemary, and fines herbes in a large bowl, tossing to combine.

Spoon the coated olives into the sterilized containers.

Whisk the vinegar into the olive oil, and then pour the mixture over the olives in each jar. Cover and refrigerate for at least 1 week before serving or giving.

Tapenade

UTENSILS NEEDED: Heavy-bottomed saucepan;
four 8-ounce containers with lids, sterilized

COOKING TIME: Approximately 20 minutes

QUANTITY: Four 8-ounce containers

STORAGE: Refrigerate in an airtight container up to 3 weeks.

SERVING SUGGESTIONS: Use as a condiment for meat, poultry, or fish; as a dip for
crudités; or as a topping for croutons, baguette slices, or sliced cooked potatoes.

Heat the olive oil in a heavy-bottomed saucepan over medium heat. Add the onion and garlic and sauté for 5 minutes, or until just beginning to color. Add the red, yellow, and green bell peppers and sauté for another 10 minutes, or just until the peppers soften. Stir in the olives, walnuts, parsley, and basil. When well blended, add the vinegar and season with salt and pepper. Bring to a boil, then lower the heat and simmer for 5 minutes.

Remove from the heat and pack the mixture into the sterilized containers. Spoon 1 tablespoon extra-virgin olive oil on the top of the mixture in each container. Cover and set aside to cool before refrigerating.

INGREDIENTS

¾ cup fine-quality olive oil

¼ cup finely chopped onion

2 tablespoons minced garlic

1 cup chopped red bell pepper

1 cup chopped yellow bell pepper

1 cup chopped green bell pepper

2 cups chopped imported black olives

1½ cups finely chopped walnuts

⅓ cup minced fresh flat-leaf parsley

2 tablespoons minced fresh basil

½ cup red wine vinegar

Coarse salt and freshly ground pepper, to taste

¼ cup extra-virgin olive oil

9

VINAIGRETTES, SALAD DRESSINGS, CONDIMENTS & SEASONINGS

VINAIGRETTES ARE A COMBINATION OF OILS, vinegars or other acids, and seasonings. For salad dressings, eggs, creams, and cheeses are added to the vinaigrette base. Not only are these sauces used to flavor both fruit and vegetable salads, but they are also used to dress pastas and vegetables as well as season meats, poultry, and fish. Depending on the additions to the base, the acidic content of vinaigrettes and dressings generally allows them to be stored for short periods at room temperature and for fairly long periods under refrigeration.

Condiments are thick and saucelike and are made of finely chopped or cooked vegetables or fruits. The base ingredients are often cooked with vinegars or other acids, along with pungent seasonings like chiles, peppers, herbs, or spices. They are most often served as sandwich or vegetable dressings or as a garnish for meats, poultry, fish, or game. Condiments can either be vacuum-sealed as directed on page 86 or stored in an airtight container in the refrigerator for a couple of months.

Seasonings can take many forms—a spice mix, seasoned vegetables and aromatics, flavored oils and vinegars, and so forth. They are used to add zest or savor to salads, vegetables, or meat, poultry, game, or fish dishes. Seasonings are usually easy to prepare and can be stored at room temperature unless otherwise directed in a specific recipe.

Almost all of these homemade foods may be packed for gift giving in recycled and reusable containers—wine or imported glass soft drink bottles, imported olive oil and vinegar bottles, and fancy gourmet condiment and seasoning jars are just a few of the materials I recycle for this purpose. They can all go together to fill great gift baskets. In the summer, I often pack some vinaigrettes, salad dressings, or vinegars and oils into a basket of farm-fresh lettuces or vegetables, or pack some condiments with barbecue tools or garnishes. I often make a gift packet of a few seasonings along with instructions for their use or add a dish or container that reflects the culinary heritage of the seasonings.

Citrus Vinaigrette

NO COOKING

UTENSILS NEEDED: Blender; six 16-ounce glass or ceramic containers with lids, sterilized

QUANTITY: Six 16-ounce containers

STORAGE: Refrigerate in an airtight container up to 2 months.

SERVING SUGGESTIONS: Use as a dressing for salad greens, cooked vegetables, grain salads, fish, or poultry.

___

Combine the grapefruit, orange, and lemon juices in a blender with the honey, tarragon, and thyme. Process to blend. With the motor running, slowly pour in the olive and extra-virgin olive oils, processing to emulsify. Season with salt and pepper. If necessary, add more honey to taste.

Pour into sterilized jars, cover, and refrigerate.

INGREDIENTS

4 cups freshly squeezed
red grapefruit juice

1 cup freshly squeezed
orange juice

½ cup freshly squeezed
lemon juice

½ to ¾ cup honey, or to taste

1 teaspoon chopped fresh
tarragon

1 teaspoon chopped fresh
thyme

4 cups olive oil

2 cups extra-virgin olive oil

Coarse salt and freshly
ground pepper, to taste

Balsamic Vinaigrette

NO COOKING

UTENSILS NEEDED: Blender; seven 16-ounce glass or ceramic containers with lids, sterilized

QUANTITY: Seven 16-ounce containers

STORAGE: Keep at room temperature in an airtight container up to 2 months.

SERVING SUGGESTIONS: Use as a dressing for salad greens, vegetables, grilled poultry, fish, or pork.

___

Combine the balsamic and red wine vinegars with the mustard in a blender. Process to just blend. With the motor running, slowly pour in the olive and canola oils, processing to emulsify. Season with salt and pepper.

Pour into sterilized containers, cover, and store at room temperature.

NOTE: If a more intensely flavored vinaigrette is desired, 1 tablespoon chopped fresh basil, rosemary, or thyme can be added to each jar.

INGREDIENTS

6 cups balsamic vinegar

½ cup red wine vinegar

3 tablespoons Dijon
mustard

5 cups olive oil

3 cups canola oil

Coarse salt and freshly
ground pepper, to taste

Miso Vinaigrette

INGREDIENTS

*1 cup white miso paste
(see Note)*

*3 cups rice wine vinegar
(see Note)*

½ cup mirin (see Note)

¼ cup tamari (see Note)

*2 tablespoons ginger juice
(see page 20)*

*1 tablespoon freshly
grated orange zest*

*Freshly ground black
pepper, to taste*

3 cups canola oil

*3 tablespoons toasted
sesame oil (see Note)*

*Coarse salt, to taste,
optional*

UTENSILS NEEDED: Blender; four 16-ounce glass or ceramic containers
with lids, sterilized

QUANTITY: Four 16-ounce containers

STORAGE: Refrigerate in an airtight container up to 2 months.

SERVING SUGGESTIONS: Use as a salad dressing for bitter greens or vegetables
and as a sauce for cold noodles, fish, pork, or poultry.

In a blender, combine the miso with the vinegar, mirin, tamari, ginger juice, orange zest, and pepper. Process to blend. With the motor running, slowly pour in the canola and sesame oils, processing to emulsify. Taste and, if necessary, adjust seasoning with salt.

Pour into sterilized jars, cover, and refrigerate.

NOTE: Miso paste, rice wine vinegar, mirin, tamari, and toasted sesame oil are available at Asian markets, some specialty food stores, and some supermarkets.

Blueberry Catsup

UTENSILS NEEDED: Heavy-bottomed saucepan; blender, optional; for preserving, four 8-ounce canning jars with lids, sterilized; for refrigerating, four 8-ounce containers with lids, sterilized

COOKING TIME: Approximately 20 minutes

QUANTITY: Four 8-ounce jars

STORAGE: Vacuum-sealed jars last 1 year; refrigerated, up to 3 months.

SERVING SUGGESTIONS: Use as a condiment for meat, fish, or vegetables, or as a seasoning for sauces.

INGREDIENTS

6 cups blueberries, washed and dried

3 cups sugar

1 cup minced red onion

¾ cups blueberry or raspberry vinegar

1 tablespoon freshly squeezed lemon juice

1 tablespoon ground cinnamon

2 teaspoons ground cloves

1 teaspoon freshly ground black pepper

Tabasco sauce, to taste

Coarse salt, to taste

Combine the blueberries, sugar, onion, vinegar, lemon juice, cinnamon, cloves, pepper, and Tabasco in a heavy-bottomed saucepan over medium-high heat. Bring to a boil, then lower the heat and simmer, stirring frequently, for about 20 minutes, or until the berries are disintegrated and the catsup is quite thick. Season with salt to taste.

(If you'd like a smooth catsup, remove the mixture from the heat and place in a blender, processing to a smooth consistency. Transfer to a clean saucepan and return to medium heat. Cook, stirring constantly, just until the mixture begins to bubble. Remove from the heat and proceed with the recipe.)

Remove from the heat and immediately pour into sterilized jars, cover, and vacuum-seal as directed on page 86, or pour into containers and refrigerate.

Red Chile Salsa

NO COOKING

UTENSILS NEEDED: Food processor fitted with the metal blade; four 8-ounce nonreactive containers with lids, sterilized

QUANTITY: Four 8-ounce containers

STORAGE: Refrigerate in an airtight container up to 3 days.

SERVING SUGGESTIONS: Use as a dip for tortilla chips or as a condiment for Mexican or Southwestern entrées.

Place the tomatillos, tomatoes, chiles, scallions, red onion, cilantro, bell pepper, garlic, and lime and orange juices in the bowl of a food processor fitted with the metal blade. Pulse to make a chunky salsa. Season with salt and pepper.

Transfer to sterilized, nonreactive containers, cover, and refrigerate.

NOTE: Instead of using a food processor, you can chop everything by hand. For a finished, restaurant look, cut the tomatillos, tomatoes, onions, and bell pepper into ¼-inch dice, finely mince the chiles and garlic, finely chop the scallions and cilantro, and then combine the vegetables with the remaining ingredients.

This salsa can also be cooked in a nonreactive saucepan over medium heat for 15 minutes and used as a sauce for meat, poultry, or fish.

INGREDIENTS

8 tomatillos, husked and quartered

3 very ripe tomatoes, cored, seeded, and peeled

1 to 2 red hot chiles, with stems, seeds, and membranes removed, or to taste

½ cup chopped scallions

½ cup chopped red onion

½ cup chopped cilantro

¼ cup chopped red bell pepper

1 tablespoon chopped garlic

1 tablespoon fresh lime juice

1 tablespoon fresh orange juice

Coarse salt and freshly ground pepper, to taste

Hot and Sweet Mustard

2 cups dry mustard
    powder, such as
    Colman's

¾ cup mustard seeds

½ cup light brown sugar

2 teaspoons roasted garlic
    purée (see page 20)

1 teaspoon minced fresh
    tarragon leaves

1 teaspoon freshly grated
    horseradish

¼ teaspoon ground cloves

¼ teaspoon ground
    allspice

½ cup beer

½ cup water

½ cup apple cider vinegar

¼ teaspoon hot sauce

Coarse salt, to taste,
    optional

½ cup honey

UTENSILS NEEDED: Nonstick saucepan; food processor fitted with a metal blade;
six 4-ounce containers with lids, sterilized

COOKING TIME: Approximately 17 minutes

QUANTITY: Six 4-ounce containers

STORAGE: Refrigerate in an airtight container up to 3 months.

Combine the dry mustard, mustard seeds, brown sugar, garlic purée, tarragon, horseradish, cloves, and allspice in a nonstick saucepan over medium heat. Add the beer, water, vinegar, and hot sauce and cook, stirring frequently, for about 7 minutes, or until the mixture comes to a boil. Lower the heat and simmer for 10 minutes more. Stir in salt, if using, and remove from the heat.

Pour the mixture into the bowl of a food processor fitted with a metal blade and, with the motor running, slowly add the honey. Process for about 1 minute, or until the mixture is well blended and slightly thickened. Pour into sterilized containers, cover, and refrigerate.

Homemade Vinegar

NO COOKING

UTENSILS NEEDED: 1-gallon glass jar with plastic or other noncorrosive lid, sterilized; wooden spoon; slotted spoon, sterilized; fine-mesh sieve lined with cheesecloth; storage jar(s) with noncorrosive lids, sterilized, number dependent on amount of wine used

RESTING TIME: 4 weeks or more

QUANTITY: Dependent on amount of wine used

STORAGE: Refrigerate in an airtight container up to 6 months.

INGREDIENTS

Up to 3 quarts red, white, or sherry wine with 10% alcohol by volume (leftover wine is fine)

1 part vinegar starter culture to 2 parts wine (see Note)

Place the wine in the glass jar and, using a wooden spoon, stir for 2 minutes to aerate it. Add the vinegar culture in the correct ratio. Cover and place in a cool, absolutely dark spot to ferment for 4 weeks.

Taste the vinegar. If it is not acidic enough for your taste, return it to the cool, dark spot and ferment for another week. If still not to your liking, continue the fermentation process until the right degree of acidity is reached.

Using a sterilized slotted spoon, lift the culture from the vinegar. Pour the vinegar through a fine-mesh sieve lined with cheesecloth.

Pour the vinegar into sterilized glass containers with noncorrosive lids and refrigerate.

NOTE: Vinegar starter culture is available from wine-making supply stores, or contact Vinegar Connoisseurs International (see Resources, page 170).

Three Flavored Vinegars

UTENSILS NEEDED: Nonreactive saucepan; fine-mesh sieve lined with cheesecloth;
four 8-ounce glass containers with noncorrosive lids, sterilized

COOKING TIME: Approximately 5 minutes

INFUSION TIME: 24 hours

QUANTITY: Four 8-ounce containers

STORAGE: Keep in an airtight container at room temperature
up to 1 month; refrigerated, up to 6 months.

INGREDIENTS

4 cups fine-quality white
wine, champagne, or
rice wine vinegar

AND

4 cups crushed fresh
berries (blueberries,
raspberries,
blackberries, etc.)

¼ cup sugar

One 3 × 2-inch strip
orange peel

A few fresh berries,
washed and dried, for
each container

OR

10 cloves garlic, peeled
and crushed, or 1 cup
minced shallots

1 teaspoon crushed red
pepper flakes

A few peeled garlic cloves
or large pieces of
shallot for each
container

OR

1 cup minced fresh
tarragon, sage, thyme,
basil, or chives, or a
combination of minced
fresh herbs, plus 8
sprigs of chosen herb(s)

Combine the vinegar with the fruit, sugar, and orange peel *or* the garlic or shallots and red pepper flakes *or* the herbs in a nonreactive saucepan. Cook over medium heat for about 5 minutes, or until the mixture comes to a boil, then remove from the heat and set aside to infuse for 24 hours.

Strain the vinegar through a fine-mesh sieve lined with cheesecloth into a clean, nonreactive saucepan. Place over medium heat and bring to a simmer.

Immediately pour the vinegar into sterilized containers, add the additional berries, garlic or shallots, or herbs, cover, and set aside to cool before storing or refrigerating.

Provençal Oil

NO COOKING

INGREDIENTS

16 cloves garlic, peeled

12 sprigs fresh thyme

12 sprigs fresh rosemary

*1 tablespoon crushed
red pepper flakes,
or to taste*

*8 cups fine-quality or
extra-virgin olive oil*

UTENSILS NEEDED: Four 16-ounce glass jars
with lids, sterilized

INFUSION TIME: 3 weeks

QUANTITY: Four 16-ounce jars

STORAGE: Keep in an airtight container in a cool,
dark spot up to 3 months.

SERVING SUGGESTION: Use as a replacement
for olive oil in any recipe.

Place 4 garlic cloves, 3 sprigs each of thyme and rosemary, and an equal portion of the red pepper flakes in each sterilized container. Add olive oil to fill each jar. Cover and set aside in a cool, dark spot to infuse for 3 weeks before serving or giving.

Ras al Hanout

NO COOKING

UTENSILS NEEDED: Spice grinder; resealable plastic bag or glass jar with lid (see Note)

QUANTITY: Approximately 1½ cups

STORAGE: Keep in an airtight container set in a cool, dry spot up to 6 months.

SERVING SUGGESTIONS: Use as a seasoning for Moroccan tagines and other
Mediterranean stews and grain dishes or for grilled meats and poultry.

INGREDIENTS

30 bay leaves

¼ cup freshly grated nutmeg

¼ cup whole cloves

¼ cup chopped cinnamon stick

¼ cup white peppercorns

¼ cup dried thyme

1 tablespoon ground allspice

Combine the bay leaves, nutmeg, cloves, cinnamon stick, peppercorns, thyme, and allspice in a medium bowl. In batches, process to a fine powder in a spice grinder.

Transfer to a resealable plastic bag or glass jar with lid, seal, and store in a cool, dry spot.

NOTE: I store Ras al Hanout in a single container and then transfer it to small containers–1 ounce or less–for giving.

Seasoned Salt

INGREDIENTS

2 cups coarse sea salt

2 teaspoons paprika

1 teaspoon dry mustard powder

1 teaspoon crushed dried rosemary

½ teaspoon dried oregano

½ teaspoon dried thyme

½ teaspoon onion powder

¼ teaspoon garlic powder

UTENSILS NEEDED: Mixing bowl; 12-ounce container with lid or resealable plastic bag (see Note)

QUANTITY: Approximately 2½ cups

STORAGE: Keep in an airtight container set in a cool, dry spot up to 6 months.

SERVING SUGGESTIONS: Use as a seasoning for grilled and roasted meats, poultry, and fish, and as a savory seasoning for popcorn.

Combine the salt with the paprika, mustard powder, rosemary, oregano, thyme, and onion and garlic powders in a mixing bowl. Stir to blend well.

Transfer to an airtight container and store as directed.

NOTE: I store this salt in a single container and transfer it to 2-ounce containers for giving.

Brandied Pepper

NO COOKING

UTENSILS NEEDED: Nonstick baking pan; 12-ounce container with lid or
resealable plastic bag (see Note)

SETTING TIME: Approximately 2 days

QUANTITY: Approximately 2½ cups

STORAGE: Keep in an airtight container set in a cool, dry spot up to 6 months.

SERVING SUGGESTIONS: Use in place of regular pepper for seasoning meat, game,
or poultry and as a crust for grilled steaks or hamburgers.

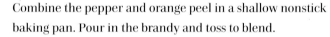

INGREDIENTS

*2 pounds cracked black
pepper (see Note)*

*¼ cup dried orange peel
(see Note)*

4 cups brandy

Combine the pepper and orange peel in a shallow nonstick
baking pan. Pour in the brandy and toss to blend.

Cover lightly with plastic film and set aside for about
2 days, or until the pepper has absorbed all of the brandy.

Transfer to an airtight container and store as directed.

NOTE: Cracked black pepper and dried orange peel are
available at most supermarkets and specialty food stores.

I store this pepper in a large container and transfer it
to 2-ounce containers for giving.

SAVORY SAUCES

10

SAVORY SAUCES ARE EITHER DRESSINGS FOR OR ACCENTS TO vegetables, meats or poultry, pastas, or grains. They are the perfect choice when you want to add flavor and provide richness, color, moisture, or an ethnic slant to a dish. They are particularly welcome homemade gifts, since many of them can quickly and easily transform a simple supper into an unexpected gourmet meal.

The sauces I have gathered come from a variety of cuisines, but don't restrict yourself to just these examples. You can certainly take almost any savory sauce that is a personal favorite and turn it into a homemade gift. Just remember that if it's an exotic ethnic sauce, it's best to label it with suggested uses, since there is nothing more dispiriting than receiving a food gift that you have no idea how to use.

Most of these sauces freeze well. Those that don't–usually the ones with lots of fresh herbs, which lose color and flavor when frozen–are generally fairly good keepers under refrigeration.

Savory sauces can be prepared for gift giving quite simply by tying a "what to do with" tag around the jar with a pretty ribbon, but I like to, when possible, place them in a container that reflects their culinary history or their use. I also like to pack two or three together to offer the recipient an easy tour around the world kitchen.

Thai Peanut Sauce

Asian Barbecue Sauce

Rouille

Charmoula

Mole Poblano

Chimichurri

Romesco Sauce

Harissa

Thai Peanut Sauce

INGREDIENTS

*2 cups creamy peanut
butter*

*2 cups canned "lite"
coconut milk*

1½ cups "lite" soy sauce

*⅔ cup freshly squeezed
orange juice*

½ cup rice wine vinegar

¼ cup sherry wine

¼ cup toasted sesame oil

*¼ cup chopped fresh
cilantro*

*2 tablespoons freshly
squeezed lime juice*

*2 tablespoons chile-garlic
sauce (see Note)*

*2 teaspoons freshly grated
ginger*

*2 teaspoons roasted garlic
purée (see page 20)*

*2 teaspoons Thai red
curry paste (see Note)*

UTENSILS NEEDED: Blender; saucepan; four 16-ounce containers with lids, sterilized

COOKING TIME: Approximately 5 minutes

QUANTITY: Four 16-ounce containers

STORAGE: Refrigerate in an airtight container up to 1 month, or freeze up to 3 months.

SERVING SUGGESTIONS: Use as a sauce for hot or cold noodles, chicken, or pork,
and as a dipping sauce.

———————

Combine all of the ingredients in a blender and process until smooth. Transfer to a saucepan and place over medium heat. Heat, stirring constantly, for about 5 minutes, or until the mixture comes to a simmer.

Remove from the heat and pour the sauce into sterilized containers, cover, and refrigerate or freeze. If frozen, blend to reincorporate after thawing.

NOTE: Chile-garlic sauce and Thai red curry paste are available at Asian markets, specialty food stores, and some supermarkets.

Asian Barbecue Sauce

UTENSILS NEEDED: Large nonreactive saucepan; whisk;
five 16-ounce containers with lids, sterilized

COOKING TIME: Approximately 15 minutes

QUANTITY: Five 16-ounce containers

STORAGE: Refrigerate in an airtight container up to 3 weeks, or freeze up to 6 months.

SERVING SUGGESTIONS: Use as a barbecue sauce for poultry, pork, and fatty fish,
and as a dressing for grain salads.

---

4 cups mango purée

4 cups mango nectar

½ cup onion purée (about 1 small onion)

¼ cup puréed roasted hot red chiles (about 4 chiles), or to taste (see page 20)

¼ cup freshly grated ginger

¼ cup freshly squeezed lime juice

¼ cup minced fresh cilantro

2 tablespoons minced fresh basil leaves

2 tablespoons cane sugar syrup or molasses

½ cup canola oil

Coarse salt and freshly ground pepper, to taste

Combine the mango purée and nectar in a large nonreactive saucepan over medium heat. Whisk in the puréed onion and chiles, ginger, lime juice, cilantro, basil, and cane syrup and bring to a simmer. Cook at a low simmer for 10 minutes. Whisk in the oil, season with salt and pepper, and cook for an additional 5 minutes.

Remove from the heat and pour into sterilized containers, cover, and refrigerate or freeze.

Rouille

INGREDIENTS

*3 dried red hot chiles,
stemmed and seeded*

*4 red bell peppers,
roasted, peeled,
cored, and seeded*

¼ cup chopped garlic

*1 teaspoon saffron
softened in
1 tablespoon
boiling water*

*1 cup fresh white bread
crumbs*

*4 large egg yolks, at room
temperature (see Note)*

*4 cups extra-virgin
olive oil*

*Coarse salt and freshly
ground pepper,
to taste*

NO COOKING

UTENSILS NEEDED: Heatproof bowl; food processor fitted with the metal blade;
eight 8-ounce glass or ceramic containers with lids, sterilized

QUANTITY: Eight 8-ounce containers

STORAGE: Refrigerate in an airtight container up to 1 week, or freeze up to 6 months.

SERVING SUGGESTIONS: Use as a seasoning for fish soups and stews, as a garnish for
large croutons, and as a flavoring for vegetables, grain salads, and pastas.

Place the dried chiles in a heatproof bowl with boiling water to cover. Set aside to soften for
15 minutes. Drain well.

Combine the roasted bell peppers, garlic, and saffron, along with its soaking water, with the softened chiles in the bowl of a food processor fitted with the metal blade. Process until smooth. With the
motor running, add the bread crumbs and blend to make a thick paste. With the motor still running,
add the egg yolks one at a time, and then slowly pour in the olive oil, processing until well emulsified.

Taste, and, if necessary, adjust the seasoning
with salt and pepper.

Transfer to sterilized containers, cover,
and refrigerate or freeze.

NOTE: If you are concerned with the safety of
consuming raw eggs, simply microwave the finished sauce for 1 minute before placing into
containers.

Charmoula

UTENSILS NEEDED: Food processor fitted with the metal blade; nonreactive saucepan;
four 8-ounce containers with lids, sterilized

COOKING TIME: Approximately 10 minutes

QUANTITY: Four 8-ounce containers

STORAGE: Refrigerate in an airtight container up to 2 weeks.

SERVING SUGGESTION: Use as a sauce for pasta, grains, shellfish, poultry, or pork.

Combine the garlic, parsley, cilantro, water, lemon juice, and orange zest in the bowl of a food processor fitted with the metal blade. Process to a smooth purée.

Scrape the herb mixture into a nonreactive saucepan. Add the oil, vinegar, tomato paste, cumin, and paprika and cook, stirring constantly, for about 5 minutes, or until the mixture comes to a simmer. Add cayenne and salt to taste, loosely cover and simmer, stirring occasionally, for 5 minutes, adding up to ½ cup water if the mixture seems too thick. (It should have a saucelike consistency.)

Remove from the heat, pour into sterilized containers, cover, and refrigerate.

INGREDIENTS

*One whole head garlic or
at least 16 cloves,
peeled*

*2 cups flat-leaf parsley
leaves*

*2 cups fresh cilantro
leaves*

1 cup water

*¼ cup freshly squeezed
lemon juice*

*2 tablespoons freshly
grated orange zest*

*1½ cups extra-virgin olive
oil*

¼ cup red wine vinegar

¼ cup tomato paste

*1½ tablespoons toasted
ground cumin*

*1½ tablespoons sweet
paprika*

Cayenne pepper, to taste

Coarse salt, to taste

Mole Poblano

6 dried ancho chiles (see Note)

6 dried mulato chiles (see Note)

4 dried pasilla chiles (see Note)

2 cups boiling water

3 medium tomatoes, peeled, cored, seeded, and chopped

2 medium onions, chopped

2 corn tortillas, chopped

2 whole cloves

1 cup blanched almonds

½ cup blanched peanuts

½ cup seedless raisins

2 tablespoons toasted sesame seeds

2 tablespoons minced garlic

½ teaspoon ground coriander

½ teaspoon ground anise seeds

½ teaspoon ground cinnamon

¼ cup vegetable oil

2 cups chicken stock or canned fat-free, low-sodium broth, plus more as needed

1½ ounces unsweetened chocolate

1 tablespoon light brown sugar, or to taste

1 tablespoon coarse salt, or to taste

2 teaspoons freshly ground black pepper

UTENSILS NEEDED: Heatproof bowl; blender; large nonreactive saucepan; eight 8-ounce glass or ceramic containers with lids, sterilized

SOAKING TIME: Approximately 30 minutes

COOKING TIME: Approximately 15 minutes

QUANTITY: Eight 8-ounce containers

STORAGE: Refrigerate in an airtight container up to 2 weeks, or freeze up to 6 months.

SERVING SUGGESTIONS: Use as a cooking sauce for poultry or pork, and as a base for many Mexican dishes.

Remove and discard the stems and seeds from the ancho, mulato, and pasilla chiles. Place the chiles in a heatproof bowl and add the boiling water. Set aside to soak for about 30 minutes, or until the chiles soften.

Transfer the softened chiles and the soaking water to a blender. Add the tomatoes, onions, tortillas, cloves, almonds, peanuts, raisins, sesame seeds, garlic, coriander, anise, and cinnamon and process to a purée. Set aside.

Heat the oil in a large nonreactive saucepan over medium heat. When very hot but not smoking, scrape the chile mixture

from the blender into the saucepan. Add the chicken stock, chocolate, brown sugar, salt, and pepper and cook, stirrring constantly, for about 15 minutes, or until the sauce is nicely blended. Add up to 1 cup additional chicken stock if the mixture is thicker than a thick sauce. Taste and, if necessary, add more sugar and salt to taste.

Remove from the heat and pour into the sterilized containers, cover, and refrigerate.

NOTE: Ancho, mulato, and pasilla chiles are available at Latin markets, specialty food stores, and many supermarkets and by mail order from Adriana's Caravan (see Resources, page 170).

Chimichurri

NO COOKING

UTENSILS NEEDED: Food processor fitted with the metal blade; whisk; six 4-ounce containers with lids, sterilized

QUANTITY: Six 4-ounce containers

STORAGE: Refrigerate in an airtight container up to 3 days.

SERVING SUGGESTIONS: Use as a condiment for meat, poultry, and fish, and as a seasoning for pasta and pasta salads.

INGREDIENTS

4 cups chopped fresh flat-leaf parsley

1 cup chopped scallion, white and pale green parts

¼ cup chopped fresh oregano

¼ cup chopped fresh cilantro

2 tablespoons chopped garlic

Juice and zest of 1 lemon

2 cups olive oil

⅔ cup white wine vinegar

Coarse salt, to taste

Combine the parsley, scallion, oregano, cilantro, garlic, and lemon juice and zest in the bowl of a food processor fitted with the metal blade. Pulse just until minced.

Scrape the herb mixture from the food processor bowl into a clean bowl. Whisk in the oil and vinegar and season with salt.

Transfer to sterilized containers, cover, and refrigerate.

Romesco Sauce

UTENSILS NEEDED: Medium saucepan; food processor fitted with the metal blade; nonreactive saucepan; six 8-ounce containers with lids, sterilized

COOKING TIME: Approximately 15 minutes

QUANTITY: Six 8-ounce containers

STORAGE: Refrigerate in an airtight container up to 1 week, or freeze up to 1 month.

SERVING SUGGESTIONS: Use as a sauce for pasta, poultry, meat, or fish. Combine with sour cream, yogurt, or mayonnaise to make a dipping sauce for vegetables or a dressing for salads.

INGREDIENTS

3 pounds red bell peppers, cored, seeded, and chopped

One 14½-ounce can tomatoes, well drained

2 cups chicken stock or canned nonfat, low-sodium chicken broth

1½ cups dry white bread cubes

1 cup toasted, blanched almonds

2 tablespoons roasted garlic purée (see page 20)

¼ cup extra-virgin olive oil

2 tablespoons sherry wine vinegar

Paprika, to taste

Coarse salt and freshly ground pepper, to taste

Combine the bell peppers and tomatoes with the chicken stock in a medium saucepan over medium heat. Bring to a simmer and let simmer, stirring occasionally, for about 10 minutes, or until the peppers are very soft.

Remove from the heat and pour the mixture into the bowl of a food processor fitted with the metal blade. Process to a smooth purée.

With the motor running, add the bread cubes, almonds, and garlic. When well blended, and with the motor still running, slowly add the oil and vinegar. When emulsified, add paprika, salt, and pepper.

Return the mixture to a clean nonreactive saucepan over medium heat. Bring to a simmer, stirring occasionally. Simmer for 5 minutes, then pour into sterilized containers, cover, and refrigerate or freeze.

Harissa

NO COOKING

UTENSILS NEEDED: Heatproof bowl; food processor fitted with the metal blade;
four 8-ounce glass jars or nonreactive containers with lids, sterilized

SOAKING TIME: Approximately 2 hours

QUANTITY: Four 8-ounce containers

STORAGE: Refrigerate in an airtight container up to 6 months.

SERVING SUGGESTIONS: Use as an accompaniment to couscous and
as a seasoning for soups, stews, and Middle Eastern dishes.

INGREDIENTS

2 pounds dried red hot chiles, stems and seeds removed

1 head garlic, peeled and chopped

1 tablespoon toasted mustard seeds

2½ cups extra-virgin olive oil

1 teaspoon coarse salt, or to taste

Place the chiles in a heatproof bowl. Add boiling water to cover by 1 inch and set aside to soak for about 2 hours, or until the chiles are very soft. Drain well and pat dry.

Place the soaked chiles in the bowl of a food processor fitted with the metal blade. Add the garlic and mustard seeds and, with the motor running, slowly add 2 cups of the olive oil. When well blended, add the salt and process to incorporate. Taste and, if necessary, add more salt.

Transfer the harissa to sterilized containers and pour some of the remaining olive oil on top of each jar's contents to cover. Seal and refrigerate.

Join us for drinks + Nibbles — 4pm

II

SNACKS & APPETIZERS

A LITTLE OF THIS AND A LITTLE OF THAT: All of the savories here are great to have on hand for last-minute entertaining at home or for taking along as a hostess present on any occasion. Most do not lend themselves to canning or preserving, but they are all either pretty good keepers under refrigeration or stay fresh in a dry pantry.

Each of these homemade foods can be easily packed for gift giving in wonderful and unusual reusable containers. Plus, together or separately, they make welcome gifts when packed with cocktail breads or crackers. With just a little effort, a cook can make quite an unexpected and lavish party tray by packing two or three of these on a pretty tray along with crackers, some Cured Wild Mushrooms (page 124) and Mediterranean Olives (page 126), and cocktail toothpicks and napkins.

Black Bean Hummus
Anchoiade
Caponata
Spiced Cheese Pot
Marinated Cheese

Black Bean Hummus

INGREDIENTS

*Four 1-pound cans
    black beans*

*1 cup (8 ounces) tahini
    (see Note)*

¼ cup chopped garlic

Juice of 6 lemons

*¼ cup chopped fresh
    flat-leaf parsley*

Coarse salt, to taste

NO COOKING

UTENSILS NEEDED: Fine-mesh sieve; food processor fitted with the metal blade;
four 8-ounce ceramic or glass containers with lids, sterilized

QUANTITY: Four 8-ounce containers

STORAGE: Cover tightly and refrigerate up to 10 days.

SERVING SUGGESTIONS: Use as a cocktail dip for pita toasts, crackers, or raw
vegetables, as a sandwich spread, and as a dressing for cold pasta salads.

———————————

Drain the beans through a sieve, separately reserving the liquid.

Combine the beans with the tahini and garlic in the bowl of a food processor fitted with the metal blade. Process to a smooth purée. With the motor running, add the lemon juice and enough of the reserved bean liquid to make a thick but spreadable mixture. Stir in the parsley and season with salt.

Immediately pack into sterilized containers, cover, and refrigerate.

NOTE: Tahini, which is ground sesame seed paste, is quite high in calories and fat so I sometimes replace it with enough nonfat plain yogurt to soften the texture and a bit of sesame oil to heighten the flavor. The flavor is not as rich nor the texture as thick, but it still makes a tasty dip—one that is very low in fat and calories.

Anchoïade

NO COOKING

UTENSILS NEEDED: Food processor fitted with the metal blade; six 4-ounce glass or ceramic containers with lids, sterilized

QUANTITY: Six 4-ounce containers

STORAGE: Cover tightly and refrigerate up to 1 month.

SERVING INSTRUCTIONS: Warm slightly and serve on croutons, crisp crackers, or baguette slices.

_____

Combine the anchovies, garlic purée, onion, and parsley in the bowl of a food processor fitted with the metal blade. Pulse for about 1 minute, or just until coarsely chopped. Add the vinegar and process to just combine.

Immediately pack into sterilized containers, cover, and refrigerate.

INGREDIENTS

24-ounce can anchovy fillets packed in olive oil, drained

¼ cup roasted garlic purée (see page 20)

2 tablespoons minced red onion

2 cups chopped fresh flat-leaf parsley leaves

⅔ cup red wine vinegar

Caponata

INGREDIENTS

¾ cup olive oil

1 large eggplant, washed, trimmed, and cut into 1-inch cubes

3 large yellow onions, peeled and chopped

2 large red bell peppers, washed, cored, seeded, and cubed

2 large green bell peppers, washed, cored, seeded, and cubed

3 large very ripe tomatoes, peeled, cored, seeded, and chopped

2 cups pitted green olives

1 cup toasted pine nuts

½ cup red wine vinegar

2 tablespoons sugar

¼ cup fresh lemon juice

1 tablespoon chopped fresh oregano

1 tablespoon chopped fresh basil

¼ to ½ cup capers, well drained, to taste

Coarse salt and freshly ground pepper, to taste

UTENSILS NEEDED: Large heavy-bottomed saucepan; six 16-ounce glass or ceramic containers with lids, sterilized

COOKING TIME: Approximately 55 minutes

QUANTITY: Six 16-ounce containers

STORAGE: Cover tightly and refrigerate up to 1 month.

SERVING SUGGESTIONS: Use as an appetizer with baguette toasts, as a cold or room-temperature side dish, and as part of an antipasto tray.

Heat the olive oil in a large heavy-bottomed saucepan over medium heat. Add the eggplant and sauté for about 15 minutes, or until the eggplant has absorbed much of the olive oil and has begun to soften. Stir in the onions and red and green bell peppers and continue to sauté for another 15 minutes. Add the tomatoes and continue to sauté for 10 minutes. Stir in the olives and pine nuts and lower the heat to a bare simmer.

Combine the vinegar and sugar and pour the mixture into the vegetables. Add the lemon juice, oregano, and basil and stir to combine. Continue to cook for 15 minutes, or until the mixture is very aromatic and the vegetables are soft but still hold their shape.

Stir in the capers and season with salt and pepper.

Immediately spoon into sterilized containers, cover, and refrigerate.

Spiced Cheese Pot

NO COOKING

UTENSILS NEEDED: Food processor fitted with the metal blade;
1 large or 2 small ceramic containers or crocks with lids, sterilized

QUANTITY: Approximately 4 cups

STORAGE: Refrigerate in an airtight container up to 1 month.

SERVING SUGGESTIONS: Use for cocktail tidbits with toasts or crackers, melted on
toasts, beaten into mashed potatoes, or as a filling for celery sticks and endive spears.

Place half of the cheese, along with the onion, garlic purée, chives, mustard, and
cayenne pepper, in the bowl of a food processor fitted with the metal blade
and process until smooth. With the motor running, add the sherry and
oil and process to incorporate. Add the remaining cheese and process
until very thick and smooth. If the mixture seems too thick, add
additional sherry wine, 1 tablespoon at a time, until desired
consistency is reached.

Scrape the mixture from the bowl and pack into
containers or crocks, cover, and refrigerate.

INGREDIENTS

*1 pound fine-quality
    cheddar cheese, cubed*

½ cup minced onion

*1 tablespoon roasted
    garlic purée (see
    page 20)*

*1 tablespoon minced fresh
    chives*

*1 tablespoon Dijon
    mustard*

Cayenne pepper, to taste

*½ cup dry sherry wine,
    plus more as needed*

1 tablespoon olive oil

Marinated Cheese

NO COOKING

UTENSILS NEEDED: Four 16-ounce glass containers with lids, sterilized

QUANTITY: Four 16-ounce containers

STORAGE: Cover tightly and refrigerate up to 2 months.

SERVING SUGGESTIONS: Use for appetizers or cocktail tidbits with crostini, or as a salad garnish, particularly with roasted beets and bitter greens.

INGREDIENTS

Four 8-ounce logs fresh goat's milk cheese or 2 pounds feta or fresh mozzarella cheese

20 black peppercorns

12 garlic cloves, roasted

8 large fresh sage leaves

4 dried red hot chiles

4 sprigs fresh rosemary

4 bay leaves

Approximately 6 cups extra-virgin olive oil

Cut the goat's milk cheese logs crosswise into 1-inch-thick rounds, or cut the feta or mozzarella into large cubes. Divide the cheese rounds or cubes among the sterilized jars, adding an equal number of peppercorns, roasted garlic cloves, sage leaves, chiles, rosemary sprigs, and bay leaves as you go, taking care that the flavorings are evenly dispersed throughout the jar. Pour in enough olive oil to cover the cheese by about 1 inch.

Using a table knife, work around the inside edges of the jars to dispel any air. Cover and refrigerate. Bring to room temperature before serving.

DRINKS

THESE ARE A FEW SPECIAL, FESTIVE BEVERAGES. As gifts, they are superb given alone or accompanied by homemade extras: Spiced Tea with a tea bread (pages 60–61) or Scotch Shortbread (page 48); Mexican Coffee Mix with Mexican Wedding Cakes (page 45); Limoncello with Candied Grapefruit Peel (page 80). The drinks are all easy to make and can be prepared well in advance of the gift-giving season to have on hand for that extra last-minute surprise.

Dry mixes can be packaged in resealable plastic bags or tightly covered jars, but they are most attractive when preserved in small, decorative, reusable canisters. The alcohol-based drinks are best stored in wine-type bottles, which can be purchased from craft stores and wine-making suppliers.

Chai
Spiced Tea
Mexican Coffee Mix
Coffee Liqueur
Ratafia
Limoncello

Chai

INGREDIENTS

¾ cup cardamom seeds, toasted

¼ cup whole cloves, toasted

¼ cup dried orange peel

2 teaspoons fennel seeds, toasted

4 cups powdered whole milk

1 cup light brown sugar, or to taste

1 tablespoon ground ginger

NO COOKING

UTENSILS NEEDED: Spice grinder; mixing bowl; seven 4-ounce containers with lids

QUANTITY: Seven 4-ounce containers

STORAGE: Keep in an airtight container in a cool, dry spot up to 6 months.

SERVING SUGGESTION: Add 2 tablespoons Chai to each cup when brewing a pot of tea. Strain before serving.

Combine the cardamom, cloves, orange peel, and fennel seeds in a spice grinder and process to a coarse grind. This may have to be done in batches.

Combine the spice mix with the powdered milk, brown sugar, and ginger in a mixing bowl, stirring to blend well.

Pack into containers, cover tightly, and store as directed.

Spiced Tea

NO COOKING

UTENSILS NEEDED: Mixing bowl; resealable plastic bag or small containers with lids

QUANTITY: Approximately 4 cups

STORAGE: Keep in an airtight container in a cool, dry spot up to 6 months.

Combine the tea with the orange and lemon zest in a mixing bowl. Using your fingertips, work the zest into the tea. Stir in the cinnamon, cloves, gingerroot, and pepper.

Transfer to airtight containers, cover, and store as directed.

NOTE: Dried gingerroot is available at Asian markets, some specialty food stores, and by mail order from Penzey's Spice House (see Resources, page 170).

INGREDIENTS

1 pound Earl Grey tea

¼ cup freshly grated orange zest

2 tablespoons freshly grated lemon zest

3 cinnamon sticks, broken into small pieces

½ cup whole cloves

1 tablespoon grated dried gingerroot (see Note)

½ teaspoon freshly ground white pepper

Mexican Coffee Mix

NO COOKING

UTENSILS NEEDED: Mixing bowl; six 2-ounce containers

QUANTITY: Six 2-ounce containers

STORAGE: Keep in an airtight container in a cool, dry spot up to 6 months.

SERVING SUGGESTION: Use 1 heaping tablespoon for every 1 cup hot water, hot milk, or a combination of equal parts boiling water and hot milk.

Combine the coffee and espresso powders with the cocoa, brown sugar, cinnamon, chile powder, and orange zest in a mixing bowl, stirring well to blend.

Place into containers, cover tightly, and store as directed.

INGREDIENTS

¾ cup instant coffee powder

¼ cup instant espresso powder

1 cup Dutch-process cocoa powder

1 cup light brown sugar

3 tablespoons ground cinnamon

1 tablespoon pure chile powder

1 tablespoon freshly grated orange zest

Coffee Liqueur

INGREDIENTS

3 cups sugar

2 cups boiling water

*¼ cup instant espresso
    powder*

3¼ cups vodka (a fifth)

*1 large vanilla bean, split
    open and cut crosswise
    into small pieces*

UTENSILS NEEDED: Medium saucepan; heatproof bowl; ½-gallon nonreactive container with lid; two 1-quart glass containers with lids

COOKING TIME: Approximately 10 minutes

INFUSING TIME: 3 weeks

QUANTITY: 2 quarts

STORAGE: Keep in an airtight container in a cool, dark spot up to 1 year.

In a medium saucepan, combine the sugar with 1 cup of the boiling water over medium heat. Cook, stirring constantly, for about 10 minutes, or until a thin syrup forms. Remove from the heat and set aside to cool to lukewarm.

Combine the espresso powder with the remaining 1 cup boiling water in a heatproof bowl, stirring to dissolve.

Combine the vodka with the lukewarm sugar syrup, coffee mixture, and vanilla bean in a nonreactive container. Cover and set aside to infuse for 3 weeks.

Pour the liqueur into two 1-quart bottles, cap, and store as directed.

Ratafía

NO COOKING

UTENSILS NEEDED: Vegetable peeler; two 3-quart nonreactive containers; fine-mesh sieve lined with damp cheesecloth; paper coffee filters; funnel; 2 wine-type bottles with corks or stoppers

INFUSING TIME: 8 weeks

RESTING TIME: 8 hours

QUANTITY: About 2 quarts

STORAGE: Keep in an airtight container in a cool, dark spot up to 1 year.

SERVING SUGGESTION: Serve in cordial glasses as a digestive.

INGREDIENTS

9 organic oranges, washed and dried

2 cups sugar

6 cups fine-quality brandy

1¼ cups toasted coriander seeds

Using a vegetable peeler, carefully remove the peel from the oranges, taking care not to cut off any of the bitter white pith. Juice the oranges and place the juice and the zest in a nonreactive container with a lid. Add the sugar and stir to dissolve. Add the brandy and coriander seeds.

Cover tightly and place in a cool, dark spot. Store, stirring occasionally, for 8 weeks.

Pour the infused liquid through the cheesecloth-lined sieve into a clean nonreactive container, pressing lightly to extract all of the liquid. Cover with plastic film and allow the liquid to rest for 8 hours. If there is sediment in the bottom of the bowl, carefully pour off the clear liquid into a clean container. Filter the remaining liquid through coffee filters to remove any particles that could cloud the ratafía.

Pour the clear liquid through a funnel into clean wine-type bottles. Cork and store in a cool, dark spot for up to 1 year.

Limoncello

INGREDIENTS

*5 pounds organic lemons,
washed and dried*

8 cups vodka

6 cups sugar

6 cups water

UTENSILS NEEDED: Vegetable peeler; 1-gallon glass container with lid;
saucepan; fine-mesh sieve; funnel; three 1-quart and one 16-ounce
glass containers with lids

INFUSING TIME: 1 week

COOKING TIME: Approximately 10 minutes

REFRIGERATION TIME: 1 month

QUANTITY: 3 quarts plus 1 pint

STORAGE: Keep in an airtight container in a cool, dark spot up to 1 year.

SERVING SUGGESTION: Serve chilled as a digestive.

————————

Using a vegetable peeler, remove the peel from the lemons, taking care not to cut off any of the white membrane. Reserve the lemons for another use.

Pour the vodka into a 1-gallon glass container. Add the lemon peel, cover, and set aside in a cool, dark spot to infuse for 1 week.

Combine the sugar and water in a large saucepan over medium heat and bring to a boil. Remove from the heat and set aside to cool.

When cool, add to the vodka mixture and stir to blend. Strain the mixture through a fine-mesh sieve into a clean container.

Pour the strained mixture through a funnel into three 1-quart and one 16-ounce glass containers, cover, and refrigerate for one month before serving or giving.

RESOURCES

Adriana's Caravan
Spices, chiles, and seasonings
404 Vanderbilt Avenue
Brooklyn, New York 11218
(800) 316-0820
adrianascaravan.com

The A.L. Bazzini Company
Nuts, roasted nuts and seeds, and dried fruits
200 Food Center Drive
Hunts Point Market
Bronx, New York 10474
(800) 228-0172
bazzininuts.com

The Baker's Catalogue
Specialty flours, baking ingredients, and equipment
P.O. Box 876
Norwich, Vermont 05055
(800) 827-6836
kingarthurflour.com

KitchenAid
Major and small kitchen appliances
2000 M-63 North, MD 8517
Benton Harbor, Michigan 49022
(269) 923-7310

New York Cake and Baking Distributors
Cookie cutters, bakeware, and decorating supplies
56 West 22nd Street
New York, New York 10010
(800) 94-CAKE-9; (212) 675-CAKE
nycake.com

Penzey's Spice House
Typical and exotic spices, herbs, and extracts
P.O. Box 933
Muskego, Wisconsin 53150
(800) 741-7787
penzeys.com

Tropical Nut & Fruit
Dried fruits, nuts, and chocolate
P.O. Box 7507
1100 Continental Boulevard
Charlotte, North Carolina 28273
(800) 438-4470
tropicalnutandfruit.com

Vinegar Connoisseurs International
Vinegar-making materials
P.O. Box 41
104 West Carlton Avenue
Roslyn, South Dakota 57261
(800) 342-4519
vinegarman.com

INDEX

CONVERSION CHART

EQUIVALENT IMPERIAL AND METRIC MEASUREMENTS

American cooks use standard containers, the 8-ounce cup and a tablespoon that takes exactly 16 level fillings to fill that cup level. Measuring by cup makes it very difficult to give weight equivalents, as a cup of densely packed butter will weigh considerably more than a cup of flour. The easiest way therefore to deal with cup measurements in recipes is to take the amount by volume rather than by weight. Thus the equation reads:

1 cup = 240 ml = 8 fl. oz.   ½ cup = 120 ml = 4 fl. oz.

It is possible to buy a set of American cup measures in major stores around the world.

In the States, butter is often measured in sticks. One stick is the equivalent of 8 tablespoons. One tablespoon of butter is therefore the equivalent to ½ ounce/15 grams.

LIQUID MEASURES

Fluid Ounces	U.S.	Imperial	Milliliters
	1 teaspoon	1 teaspoon	5
¼	2 teaspoons	1 dessertspoon	10
½	1 tablespoon	1 tablespoon	14
1	2 tablespoons	2 tablespoons	28
2	¼ cup	4 tablespoons	56
4	½ cup		120
5		¼ pint or 1 gill	140
6	¾ cup		170
8	1 cup		240
9			250, ¼ liter
10	1¼ cups	½ pint	280
12	1½ cups		340
15		¾ pint	420
16	2 cups		450
18	2¼ cups		500, ½ liter
20	2½ cups	1 pint	560
24	3 cups		675
25		1¼ pints	700
27	3½ cups		750
30	3¾ cups	1½ pints	840
32	4 cups or 1 quart		900
35		1¾ pints	980
36	4½ cups		1000, 1 liter
40	5 cups	2 pints or 1 quart	1120

SOLID MEASURES

U.S. AND IMPERIAL MEASURES		METRIC MEASURES	
Ounces	Pounds	Grams	Kilos
1		28	
2		56	
3½		100	
4	¼	112	
5		140	
6		168	
8	½	225	
9		250	¼
12	¾	340	
16	1	450	
18		500	½
20	1¼	560	
24	1½	675	
27		750	¾
28	1¾	780	
32	2	900	
36	2¼	1000	1
40	2½	1100	
48	3	1350	
54		1500	1½

OVEN TEMPERATURE EQUIVALENTS

Fahrenheit	Celsius	Gas Mark	Description
225	110	¼	Cool
250	130	½	
275	140	1	Very Slow
300	150	2	
325	170	3	Slow
350	180	4	Moderate
375	190	5	
400	200	6	Moderately Hot
425	220	7	Fairly Hot
450	230	8	Hot
475	240	9	Very Hot
500	250	10	Extremely Hot

Any broiling recipes can be used with the grill of the oven, but beware of high-temperature grills.

EQUIVALENTS FOR INGREDIENTS

all-purpose flour—plain flour
baking sheet—oven tray
buttermilk—ordinary milk
cheesecloth—muslin
coarse salt—kitchen salt
cornstarch—cornflour

eggplant—aubergine
granulated sugar—caster sugar
half-and-half—12% fat milk
heavy cream—double cream
light cream—single cream
parchment paper—greaseproof paper

plastic wrap—cling film
scallion—spring onion
shortening—white fat
unbleached flour—strong, white flour
zest—rind
zucchini—courgettes or marrow